MY GRAMMAR AND I
(OR SHOULD THAT BE 'ME'?)

Caroline Taggart is a freelance writer and editor. She is the editor and spokesperson for *Writer's Market UK*, an annual guide for aspiring writers, and also enjoyed (immensely) a stint as a bestselling author following the publication of *I Used to Know That: Stuff You Forgot from School.*

J. A. Wines is a freelance writer, compiler and editor. Her other works include *The Book of Garden Games, Dogs' Miscellany* and, most recently, *Mondegreens: A Book of Mishearings.*

MY GRAMMAR AND I

(OR SHOULD THAT BE 'ME'?)

OLD-SCHOOL WAYS TO SHARPEN YOUR ENGLISH

CAROLINE TAGGART AND J. A. WINES

MICHAEL O'MARA BOOKS LIMITED

Revised paperback edition first published in 2011

First published in Great Britain in 2008 by
Michael O'Mara Books Limited
9 Lion Yard, Tremadoc Road
London SW4 7NQ

Papers used by Michael O'Mara Books Limited are natural, recyclable
products made from wood grown in sustainable forests. The manufacturing
processes conform to the environmental regulations of the country of origin.

A CIP catalogue record for this book is available from the British Library.

ISBN 978-1-84317-657-2

17 19 20 18

www.mombooks.com

Text design and typesetting by Glen Saville
Printed and bound by CPI Group (UK) Ltd, Croydon, CR0 4YY

CONTENTS

Acknowledgements 7
Introduction: A very brief history of English grammar 8
Grammar rules (to avoid). 12

1. SPELLING AND CONFUSABLES. 13
ABC: Easy as 123 (or, Spelling) 14
That which comes before (or, Prefixes) 29
Happy endings (or, Suffixes) 31
That's capital (or, Capitalization). 33
Countdown (or, Vowels and consonants) 34

2. PARTS OF SPEECH 36
Say what? (or, Parts of speech). 37
Definitely indefinite (or, Articles) 39
Demonstrate your determination (or, Determiners) 44
What's in a name? (or, Nouns) 46
One die, two dice (or, Singular and plural) 53
Thou and thee (or, Pronouns) 62
What a to-do (or, Verbs) 70
Kind of funny-looking (or, Adjectives). 90
Reverently, discreetly, advisedly, soberly... (or, Adverbs) . . 93
Dangly bits (or, Misplaced modifiers) 98
May I compare thee to a summer's day? (or, Comparatives) . 100
And now we'll move on (or, Conjunctions) 103
It's behind you! (or, Prepositions) 108
Holy moly! (or, Interjections). 115

3. SENTENCE STRUCTURE 116

Do I get time off for good behaviour? (or, Sentences) 117

Subject Verb Object. 122

On the subject of I and the object of me

(or, Subject and object) 126

Don't you agree? (or, Agreement) 132

From major to minor (or, Clauses). 137

How do you phrase that? (or, Phrases). 142

4. PUNCTUATION 144

Stop! (or, Full stops). 145

Take a deep breath (or, Commas) 148

What is this, the Spanish Inquisition?

(or, Question marks) 156

Something to shout about (or, Exclamation marks). 159

Two pricks (or, Colons) 161

Supercomma to the rescue (or, Semicolons) 162

Dash it all! (or, Dashes) 163

Joined-up writing (or, Hyphens) 165

'Quotation marks'. 166

What's all the fuss? (or, Apostrophes) 168

What's not in a name? (or, Possessive apostrophes) 170

5. ODDS AND SODS (OR, ELEMENTS OF STYLE)177

Being a bit fancy 178

A big no-no (or, Double negatives). 178

Pleonasm, prolixity and tautology (or, Wordiness). 182

Bibliography. 190

ACKNOWLEDGEMENTS

Thanks to Silvia for sillinesses; to Glen for making sense of it all; to Cec, who knows more about this subject than Calvin Coolidge put together; and to everyone who valiantly stayed conscious while we tried to discuss grammar with them.

INTRODUCTION:
A VERY BRIEF HISTORY OF
ENGLISH GRAMMAR

> '[It is] impossible at the present juncture to teach
> English grammar in the schools for the simple reason
> that no one knows exactly what it is.'
> **GOVERNMENT REPORT, 1921**

Anyone who has so much as run their eye over an Anglo-Saxon lament, a tale by Chaucer or a play by Shakespeare will see that the English in which they are written is very different from the way we write and speak today. Even a novel written as little as fifty years ago may differ from a modern one in style, vocabulary and punctuation. The books of poor old Enid Blyton, most of which were written in the 1940s and 1950s, have already had to be revised for modern children because they were considered so out of touch – and not least because she had a propensity for naming her characters Fanny, Dick and so on.

It is in the nature of a living language to evolve, as new inventions require new words, foreign influences enliven the vocabulary and social changes give people more or less leisure to write at length. The monks who copied out medieval texts invented short forms to save themselves time, which passed into the language as ligatures in words such as, funnily enough, *mediæval*, which we now deem archaic. In our own time the great revolutions have occurred because of emailing and texting; the *Collins English Dictionary* of 2009 contains the word *gr8*.

We cannot stop English changing – and only the most ardent, dyed-in-the-wool pedants waste their time trying – but we can do our best to ensure that it does not become compromised along the way, and to preserve its best features. Since linguistic sloppiness often leads to ambiguity – which is one of the things that grammar rules try to avoid – a few rules are surely a good thing. And frankly, if you can't bring yourself to agree with that, you might as well stop reading now and go and get your money back before the book starts to look tatty.*

Rules were very much in the minds of the sticklers of the eighteenth century, who, fearing for the health of the English language, decided to impose on it a grammar system that would fix it good and proper. Unfortunately for us, these scholars were specialists in Ancient Greek and Latin – not German, the language from which English is derived – so they imposed an awful lot of Latin rules that didn't fit too comfortably with English, thereby creating all manner of unnecessary complications. Most English people couldn't even speak Latin, let alone master its grammar.

Ignoring this major flaw in the plan, in 1762, an Oxford professor called Robert Lowth produced a prescriptive text titled *A Short Introduction to English Grammar*, a publication so influential that it dominated grammar teaching into the twentieth century (and indeed is much quoted in this book). No longer did one dare to end a sentence with a preposition, to split an infinitive or to say 'between you and I'.

Lowth's rules aside, the majority of people would have had little knowledge of English grammar until the end of the nineteenth century. Most of them couldn't read or write, never mind worry

---

* Unless you are reading in the bath, in which case it is probably too late. Tough.

about un-splitting infinitives. It was not until the late 1800s that schooling became compulsory and children were sent off to learn how not to blot their copybook.

☛ **Swot's Corner:** The earliest grammar systems we know of were in Iron Age India, about the fifth century BC. The Greeks had a grammar system by 100 BC, and the Romans created a Latin grammar system following the Greek example. Some 272 grammars of English were published before the eighteenth century.

Grammar teaching was regarded as important until the early 1960s, when the authorities decided that we did not need to be drilled in a language we could already speak, and pretty much everyone decided that Latin was boring and pointless. Thirty years later, however, businesses and universities began to complain about the younger generation's bad grammar and punctuation, with the result that the subject was once again taken seriously and reappeared on school syllabuses.* But, like maths, it remains a subject that many of us regard with foreboding. Either you belong to the generation that 'missed out' on grammar when its teaching was out of fashion; or, if you are older or younger than that, you'll have hazy recollections of rules that you perhaps only half understood in the first place.

---

* *Syllabi?* Not necessarily – see p.59.

☛ **Swot's Corner:** When grammar became a required subject in many US schools in the mid-nineteenth century, teachers complained that they knew no more about it than their pupils.

This book aims to fill in some of the gaps that the education system may have left you with,* but remember that English is a rich and fluid language and that one person's unbreakable rule is another person's insufferable pedantry. Knowing the rules – and breaking them because you feel like it, not because you don't know any better – will make you a more confident, creative and entertaining writer and speaker.

If your reaction to that is along the lines of 'Yeah, right,' consider this: when you're chatting among friends, it may not much matter how you express yourself, but what about when you are applying for a job or compiling a report or trying to write an introduction for a book like this?† Language is as much a part of how you present yourself – and how other people react to you – as the way you dress. if we alwez rote howeva we pleazd itd b like turning up 2 an interview in ript jeanz n a scruffy t-shirt, y'know? And one wouldn't dream of doing that, would one?

---

* Yes, OK: *with which the education system may have left you.*
† Or should that be *such as this*? See p.23.

GRAMMAR RULES (TO AVOID)*

1. Verbs has to agree with their subjects.
2. Remember to never split an infinitive.
3. Parenthetical remarks (however relevant) are (usually) unnecessary.
4. Never use a big word when a diminutive one would suffice.
5. Use words correctly, irregardless of how others elude to them.
6. Use the apostrophe in it's proper place and omit it when its not needed.
7. Eliminate unnecessary references. As Ralph Waldo Emerson once said, 'I hate quotations.'
8. Who needs rhetorical questions?
9. Exaggeration is a billion times worse than understatement.
10. Last but not least, avoid clichés like the plague.

---

* Inspired by William Safire's 'Fumblerules', first published in the *New York Times*, 1979.

1.
SPELLING
AND CONFUSABLES

ABC:
EASY AS **123** (OR, SPELLING)

> 'My spelling is Wobbly. It's good spelling but it
> Wobbles, and the letters get in the wrong places.'
> **A. A. MILNE,** *Winnie-the-Pooh*

In the late 1500s, the state of English **spelling** and the 'invasion' of foreign words was troubling scholars and schoolteachers to the extent that some of them took it upon themselves to harness the language by compiling dictionaries. But even with the help of education and dictionaries, spelling can still be an uphill climb.

✋ **Smart Alec:** More than one-tenth of English words are not spelt the way they sound.

We have an overwhelming tendency to leave letters in words even though they are no longer pronounced (think of the *g* in *weight* or *daughter*, for example, or the *b* in *subtle*, or the *p* in *pneumonia*). And we are surely the only language to have nine ways to pronounce a single four-letter combination:

A rough-coated, dough-faced, thoughtful ploughman strode through the streets of Scarborough; after falling into a slough, he coughed and hiccoughed.

Then we have things called **eye rhymes**, which are words that look alike and perhaps used to rhyme but which, due to shifts in pronunciation, no longer do. In Shakespeare's day,

> *Blow, blow thou winter wind*
> *Thou art not so unkind*

would probably have rhymed, as would

> *I am monarch of all I survey…*
> *From the centre all round to the sea*

when Cowper wrote those lines nearly two hundred years later.

Then there is another problem. Many words that sound the same are spelled differently.

aloud/allowed	*fair/fare*	*pale/pail*
beach/beech	*knot/not*	*plane/plain*

which makes English a wonderful language for puns but a nightmare for non-native speakers and for those who aren't confident in their spelling (or who rely on their spellcheckers).

> 'They went and told the sexton, and
> The sexton toll'd the bell.'
> **THOMAS HOOD**

☝ **Smart Alec:** A **homophone** is a word that is pronounced the same as another word but differs in meaning. The words may be spelt the same or differently.

It's my bizness to be definate

Here are the correct spellings of a random selection of commonly misspelt* words:

accidentally	*cemetery*	*liaison*
accommodate	*definite*	*millennium*
allege	*diarrhoea*	*necessary*
avocado	*ecstasy*	*niece*
association	*embarrass*	*privilege*
broccoli	*grammar*	*separate*
business	*height*	*sincerely*

Take my advice

In these commonly confused noun/verb pairs, the noun has a *c* and the verb has an *s*.†

Noun	Verb
advice	*advise*
practice	*practise*
device	*devise*
prophecy	*prophesy*
licence	*license*

---

* Ironically, *misspelt* is often misspelt.
† For more on nouns and verbs, see p.46 and p.70.

Useful mnemonic: *I'd advise you not to give advice.* We find this helpful because *advice* and *advise* are pronounced differently, but the rule of *c = noun, s = verb* applies to all the others, too.

That's if you're British, by the way. If you are American, it is often, but not always, the other way round. Did we mention that spelling was an uphill climb?

🐦 **Swot's Corner:** Until the eighteenth century, English spelling was not standardized on either side of the Atlantic. Then, in 1755, Samuel Johnson published his *Dictionary of the English Language*, and in 1828 Noah Webster published *An American Dictionary of the English Language*.

Webster was an orderly-minded man who disapproved of a lot of the spelling that Johnson had recorded (indeed, he disapproved of a lot about Johnson, saying that he was 'naturally indolent and seldom wrote until he was urged by want. Hence... he was compelled to prepare his manuscripts in haste.').

Webster's dislike of words that weren't pronounced the way they looked led him to decree that words such as *centre* and *theatre* should be spelled *center* and *theater*; he also dropped the silent *u* from words such as *colour, favour* and *honour*. In fact, Webster was single-handedly responsible for most of the differences between British and American spelling that survive to this day.

Seize the sieve: a spelling rule

The most famous **spelling rule** is *'i' before 'e' except after 'c'*, although this does not work for *ancient, foreign, neither, protein, science, seize, species, vein* or lots of other words. It really applies only to certain words in which the *ie* or *ei* makes an *ee* sound: *achieve, receive, deceive.*

So even the most famous spelling rule works only in a very limited set of circumstances. Hey ho. There is really no way round this other than reading a lot, taking note of unfamiliar words and investing in a good dictionary.

One word or two?

As a general rule, one word tends to be an adjective, while two words form the noun. Here are some common confusions:

alot/a lot
There is no such word as *alot*. *A lot* of people know that *a lot* should be two words. If you mean to write the verb *allot*, however, you should allot it two *l*s.

alright/all right
Chambers Dictionary describes *alright* as an alternative, less acceptable spelling of *all right.*
Useful mnemonic: *It's either all right or all wrong.*

altogether/all together
Altogether, it's sixty miles.
All together now: *'Sixty miles to go...'*

anyone/any one
*Does this bag belong to **anyone**?*
*It could belong to **any one** of those tourists over there.**

always/all ways
*I **always** get lost in Rome.*
***All ways** lead to Rome.*

cannot/can not
Either is acceptable, but *cannot* is more common. Sometimes *can not* may be the better choice if you want to be emphatic: *No, you **can not** speak Swahili.†*

everyday/every day
*His **everyday** life is very dull, but at night he's in a cabaret act.*
***Every day** I dream of becoming a showgirl.*

everyone/every one
***Everyone** has a guilty secret.*
***Every one** of you pretends not to like Barry Manilow.*

into/in to
*I can't seem to get **into** the office.*
*I was hoping to go **in to** use the free internet.*

maybe/may be
***Maybe** you'll remember what I tell you in future.*
*Although it **may be** that I forgot to tell you in the first place.*

---

* A sign recently seen in a shop window: 'One schoolchild allowed in this shop at anyone time.' As opposed to nobody time?
† *Can* can be tricky – turn to p.76.

nobody/no body, somebody/some body, anybody/any body
Nobody was at the crime scene, so I assumed they'd all gone home.
*There was a lot of blood at the crime scene, but **no body**.*

*I think **somebody** is trying to break in.*
*Gosh, that burglar has quite **some body**.*

*Will **any body** do for the bikini advert, or does **anybody** here happen to have Pamela Anderson's contact details?*

sometimes/some times
Sometimes trains arrive on time.
Some times on that train timetable I gave you are wrong.
*I'll give you a ring **sometime**.*
*Perhaps we can arrange **some time** for ourselves.*

And one instance of 'one word or three?'

insofar/in so far
Your choice: *We agree **insofar** (or **in so far**) as your design looked wonderful; it's just that mohair tights aren't in high demand.* Both versions are perfectly acceptable.

I'll get my cloak

When two words are combined to form a single word, the new word is called a **portmanteau word**. As Humpty Dumpty tells Alice in *Through the Looking-Glass*, 'There are two meanings packed into one word.' For example:

breakfast and lunch	*brunch*
Français and Anglais	*Franglais*
guess and estimate	*guesstimate*
information and commercial	*infomercial*
motor and hotel	*motel*
smoke and fog	*smog*

✋ **Smart Alec:** *Portmanteau* is itself made up of two words, the French *porter* (to carry) and *manteau* (cloak or mantle).

What's the word I'm after?

abuse/misuse/disabuse
To *abuse* something means to treat it so badly that you damage it.
To *misuse* something means to use it wrongly.
To *disabuse* someone of something means to show them that their thinking is wrong.

acute/chronic
An *acute* illness is one that is sudden and severe but short-lived.
A *chronic* illness persists for a long time.
Useful mnemonics:
acute: children are short, a pain, and not cute for long.
chrOnic = Old (lasting a lOng time).

affect/effect
Affect is a verb and *effect* is a noun. So you *affect* something by

having an *effect* on it. (The exception is if you *effect* a change; that is, cause a change to happen.)

Useful mnemonic:

RAVEN, that is: *Remember Affect Verb Effect Noun.*

aggravate/annoy

Aggravate means 'to make worse'. Therefore, while you can *aggravate* a situation, a problem or a condition, you irritate or *annoy* people.

alternate/alternative

An alternate plan would be wrong. The verb *alternate* means going back and forth between two things, and thus you have *alternate* letters of the alphabet (a, c, e, g, etc.). If you mean 'another plan', it should be *alternative*.

among/between

Use *between* for two things; *among* for more than two.

Between you and me, there's no way we can divide these five loaves and two fishes among our five thousand guests.

Useful mnemonic:

beTween = Two

aMong = Many

amount/number

A rhyming mnemonic: *use amount for things we cannot count.*

That's a large amount of sugar for one cup of tea.

What is an acceptable number of sugars for one cup of tea?

as/like

Something looks *like* something else – they physically resemble one another.

*He looks **like** his mother and she looks **like** Margaret Thatcher.*

However:

*It looks **as if** a storm is coming.*

*Teenagers use words **such as** 'like' far too often.*

***As with** all homework, pupils can now research geography topics online.**

> 'He rose like a trout to the fly of any phrase.'
> **VIOLET ASQUITH ON WINSTON CHURCHILL**

complement/compliment

*May I **compliment** you on your new hairstyle? The colour **complements** your dress beautifully.*

Useful mnemonic:

*A compl**E**ment adds something to make it **E**nough.*

*A comp**LIME**nt puts you in the **LIME**light.*

continual/continuous

Continual means 'happening over and over and over again'; *continuous* means 'happening constantly without stopping'. You may *continually* receive unwanted telephone calls from telesales people. However, if this were happening *continuously*, you would never be able to put the phone down.

---

* ***Like** all homework, pupils...* would be a dangling modifier. Dangling what? See p.98.

Useful mnemonic:

continuAL = Able to Leave off
continuouS = never Stopping

defuse/diffuse

You *defuse* a situation, by (metaphorically) taking the *fuse* out of it before it catches fire.

Diffuse means 'to spread out' if it is a verb, or 'already spread out' if it is an adjective.

due to/owing to

This is another of those 'strictly speaking' problems. *Chambers Dictionary* says that *due to* means 'caused by' with a second definition of 'owing to, because of', which, it adds, is 'a use still deprecated by some but now almost standard'. So, for the benefit of the pedants among us:

Due to means 'caused by'.

Owing to means 'because of'.

To determine which to use, decide whether you would replace *due to* or *owing to* by *caused by* or *because of*.

*The collapse of hundreds of buildings was **due to** the earthquake.*

***Owing to** collapsed roads and bridges, it was impossible to get outside help.*

elude/allude

*Your meaning **eludes** me. I do not understand to what you are **alluding**.*

farther/further

Another one where the difference is becoming blurred, but

generally speaking *farther* relates to a physical distance, *further* to metaphorical distance.

*Before we travel any **farther**, let's have a **further** look at the map.*
*Before we take this argument any **further**, how much **farther** is it to the hotel?*

Useful mnemonic: *FARther is about how FAR.*

fortuitous/fortunate

Fortuitous means 'happening by chance', but not necessarily a *fortunate* chance.

forward/foreword
Useful mnemonic:
forwArd means to Advance.
foreword: the WORDs that come beFORE the main text.

hear/here
Useful mnemonics:
One hEARs with one's EARs.
I want HER to come HERe.

hanged/hung

Pictures or meat are *hung*; criminals used to be *hanged*.

imply/infer

Speakers *imply* something by hinting at it; listeners *infer* something based on the information they hear.

*I **infer** from your tone that you are angry with me.*
*I didn't mean to **imply** that.*

lay/lie/laid

You *lie* in bed but *lay* the table, or *lay* the book on the table or (if you are a hen) *lay* an egg.

In the past tense, you *lay* in bed all day yesterday, but you *laid* the table or the book or the egg.

So *lie* is the present tense of an intransitive verb* that means 'to put oneself or to remain in a more or less horizontal position'. The present participle is *lying*, the past tense is *lay* and past participle *lain*.

Lay is the present tense of a transitive verb whose basic meaning is 'to place something in a more or less horizontal position', the present participle is *laying*, the past tense and past participle *laid*.

In the sense of telling an untruth, the forms are *lie, lying* and *lied*.

And the concept of *an easy lay* has nothing to do with hens.

lend/loan

Lend is a verb, *loan* is normally a noun.

*If she asks me for a **loan**, I will **lend** her the money.*

Useful mnemonic:

*People will gr**OAN** if you ask them to l**OAN**.*

*People will s**END** if you ask them to l**END**.*

Though increasingly *loan* is used as a verb: *The bank will **loan** you the money if you have enough security.* Not everybody likes this, but it's in the dictionaries.

less/fewer

Ah, the scourge of supermarket sign-writers.†

Less means 'not as much'.

Fewer means 'not as many'.

---

* For more on verbs, see p.70. For more on tenses, see p.80.

† See p.48 for further ranting on this matter.

Or, if you prefer, *fewer* is used to denote things that can be counted and *less* to describe things that can't.

Never refer to *less people*. People should stand up and be counted!

loose/lose

Count the *o*s and remember: *if I **lose** any more weight, my clothes will be too **loose***.

older/elder

An *elder* is a tribesman or a tree. As an adjective, it means *older*, but it is sometimes used to denote respect: *an **elder** statesman* or even *my **elder** sister* may be assumed to have attained a certain amount of wisdom.

Older just means 'more old', the way you sometimes feel in the morning, or when you are talking to someone who's never heard of Alvin Stardust.

oral/aural/verbal

Oral pertains to the mouth, *aural* to the ears, *verbal* to words.

An *oral statement* means one that is not written down. An *oral examination* may be one that is not written down, or it may be performed by a dentist. An *oral/aural examination* may be in a foreign language to test how well you understand what you are hearing as well as how well you speak. A *verbal statement* is a tautology (how would you make it without using words?).

principal/principle
Useful mnemonic:

*The chief g**AL** is the princip**AL**; she makes ru**LE**s called princip**LE**s.*

rob/steal

You *rob* a person and *steal* a thing, but not the other way round.

Useful mnemonic:

*You can **rob** Rob, and you can **steal** steel,*
*But you can't **steal** Rob and you can't **rob** steel.*

stationary/stationery

Stationery is sold by a stationer. His shop is likely to be *stationary*.

their/there

Their means 'belonging to them'.
There means 'in that place'.

Useful mnemonic:

*They left tHEIR money to their son and **HEIR**.*
***WHERE** shall we place ourselves, **HERE** or tHERE?*

weather/whether

*I do not know **whether** he is **weather**-wise.*

> 'Whether the weather be fine,
> Whether the weather be not,
> We must weather the weather,
> Whatever the weather,
> Whether we like it or not.'
> **ANON.**

THAT WHICH COMES BEFORE (OR, PREFIXES)

A **prefix** is a group of letters that is added to the beginning of a word to change its meaning. Common ones include:

anti	*extra*	*mono*	*pseudo*
auto	*hyper*	*multi*	*re*
circum	*inter*	*omni*	*sub*
demi	*intra*	*photo*	*tele*
dis	*mega*	*pre*	*trans*

Rule: adding a prefix does not change the spelling of the original word, nor usually the spelling of the prefix, even when the last letter of the prefix and the first letter of the original word are the same: *disservice, dissimilar, unnerve, unnecessary.*

✋ **Smart Alec:** What of *dispirited*? And *transubstantiation*?
Answer: There are always exceptions. *Always* being one of them.

All's well that starts well...

Rule: when *all* and *well* are used as prefixes, take away one *l* – *altogether, welfare.* But note that this is not the case with hyphenated words: *all-embracing, well-adjusted, well-bred.*

The opposite of what I mean

The prefixes *dis-*, *il-*, *im-*, *in-*, *ir-*, *mis-* or *un-* create words that mean the opposite of the root word (*il-*, *ir-* and *im-* are all variants of *in-*, used respectively in front of words beginning with *l*, *r*, and *b*, *m* or *p*): *disobey, illogical, impossible, inapplicable, irresponsible, misunderstood, unattainable.*

But be careful when a root word can take two or more of these prefixes, as the resulting words will have subtly or completely different meanings: *Do I **disremember** or **misremember**? I can't remember.**

The loss of paid overtime left most of the workers **dis**affected. The only ones who were **un**affected by this decision were those who never worked overtime.

I collected my children's **dis**used toys, intending to donate them to the fundraiser. However, years of **mis**use had left many of them fit only for the dustbin.

He was a **dis**interested lawyer, and therefore **un**interested in taking a bribe.

---

* Hillary Clinton will never disremember nor misremember having 'misspoken' to the detriment of her 2008 election campaign, claiming falsely that she had experienced heavy artillery fire in Bosnia in 1996. 'If I misspoke it was just a misstatement,' she explained. And you can't argue with that.

HAPPY ENDINGS (OR, SUFFIXES)

Suffixes are added to the *end* of a word to change its meaning. Common ones include:

-ant	*-ise*	*-ful*
-ent	*-ist*	*-ness*
-ible	*-fy*	*-ism*
-ing	*-ly*	*-ment*
-ize	*-able*	*-ation*

Adding a suffix may alter the spelling of the preceding word. If a word ends in a *y* that is preceded by a consonant (*happy, beauty*), the *y* changes to *i*:

happy	*happiness*
beauty	*beautiful*

But if the *y* is preceded by a vowel, the *y* remains: *I envy your enjoyment of the situation. It obviously caused you much merriment.* And if the original word ends in an *e*, this is usually dropped: *You are most **lovable** but not at all **sensible**.*

✋ **Smart Alec:** Hold on to the *e* if dropping it would alter pronunciation. *Pronouncable* would be pronounced *pronounkable*, but *pronounceable* is quite *manageable*.

Actually, both *aging* and *ageing* are correct. As are *likable* and *likeable*. If anyone knows why, please don't write in.

☞ See Me After Class:

She stopped using hair irons because she kept singing her hair.
I don't think I know that tune.

Romeo was dyeing to see Juliet.
Did she insist on a new colour?

Toad was carless to wreck his car.
He was afterwards!

'-able' and '-ible'

It's not easy to remember which words end in *–able* and which in *–ible*, and there certainly isn't a hard and fast rule. Too much of it depends on the Latin root and whether the word comes to us direct from Latin or via French and wouldn't you rather just invest in a decent dictionary and look each word up as the necessity arises?

THAT'S CAPITAL (OR, CAPITALIZATION)

A **capital letter** is the Large Letter that is used at the beginning of a sentence and as the first letter of certain words. The word comes from the Latin *capitalis*, derived from *caput*, a head.

Use a capital letter...

- for the first word of a sentence
- for the first word in a line of poetry
- for the major words in the title of books, plays, films, works of art: *That's Capital, Tom Brown's Schooldays, The Catcher in the Rye, Casablanca, The Laughing Cavalier*
- for proper nouns: *James, Dad, the Queen, the President*
- for place names and the names of buildings: *London, Paris, Easy Street, the Taj Mahal, Buckingham Palace*
- for adjectives derived from proper nouns: *English, Shakespearean, Victorian*
- for the pronoun *I*
- for personal titles that come before a name: *Mr, Ms, Mrs, Dr, Captain, Reverend*
- for most letters in words that are acronyms: *NASA, NATO*
- for the months of the year, days of the week, and special occasion days: *Christmas, Easter, Thanksgiving, Happy Birthday* (but *in the new year, his birthday*

seemed to come round faster each year)
- for brand names: *Kleenex, Mars, Hoover*

Do not use a capital...
- after a colon or semicolon
- when talking about kings, queens, presidents and generals in general, rather than a specific individual
- for the seasons – *spring, summer, autumn, winter*
- for compass points: *north, south, east, west, going north, heading south*. However, do write *the South* (as in *the American Civil War was fought largely between the North and the South*), *the South Pole*

☛ **Swot's Corner:** Capital letters are sometimes referred to as 'upper case'. This is because manual typesetters kept these letters in the upper drawers of a desk – the upper-type case. More frequently used letters were stored on a lower shelf, thus 'lower case' letters.

COUNTDOWN (OR, VOWELS AND CONSONANTS)

'Always end the name of your child with a vowel, so that when you yell the name will carry.'
BILL COSBY

The word *vowel* derives from the Latin word *vox*, meaning 'voice'. The dictionary definitions of a **vowel** are a bit scary: 'a voiced speech sound whose articulation is characterized by the absence of a friction-causing obstruction in the vocal tract, allowing the breath stream free passage;' or 'a speech sound made with vibration of the vocal cords but without audible friction, more open than a consonant and capable of forming a syllable.'

Eek.

But actually, that 'capable of forming a syllable' bit is what matters. You can't form a syllable – and therefore can't make a word – without a vowel.

There are five vowels in English: *A E I O* and *U* (**useful mnemonic:** *An Elephant In Orange Underwear*). But the letter *y*, although classed as a consonant and used as one in words such as *yellow, young* and *beyond*, is often used as a vowel (with an -*i* sound) in words such as *cry, fly, lynx* and *rhythm*. In Welsh *w* is also a vowel (pronounced like the -*oo* in *room*), which is why you occasionally see such odd-looking words as *cwm* (pronounced 'coom'), meaning a steep-sided valley, and *crwth* ('krooth'), a type of stringed instrument.

Consonants, by the way, are all the letters that aren't vowels.*

---

* Oh, OK, the breath is partly obstructed when you pronounce them, and they can't make syllables on their own, but do you really care? Let's move on.

2.
PARTS
OF SPEECH

SAY WHAT?
(OR, PARTS OF SPEECH)

Every word in every language can be categorized according to its grammatical properties, which is what we mean by **parts of speech**. As with so many other things, this system was invented by the Ancient Greeks, copied by the Romans and later adopted into English by scholars who were well versed in Latin, whether it was appropriate or not. (In many cases it was not appropriate, but we're stuck with it now, and that's what this book is all about.)

In English there are generally considered to be eight parts of speech: *noun, pronoun, adjective, verb, adverb, preposition, conjunction* and *interjection*, and you may once have learnt this useful piece of doggerel to help you remember what each did:

Every name is called a NOUN,
*As **field** and **fountain**, **street** and **town**;*

In place of noun the PRONOUN stands
*As **he** and **she** can clap **their** hands;*

The ADJECTIVE describes a thing,
*As **magic** wand and **bridal** ring;*

The VERB means action, something done —
***To read, to write, to jump, to run**;*

How things are done, the ADVERBS tell,
*As **quickly, slowly, badly, well**;*

> *The PREPOSITION shows relation,*
> *As **in** the street, or **at** the station;*
>
> *CONJUNCTIONS join, in many ways,*
> *Sentences, words, **or** phrase **and** phrase;*
>
> *The INTERJECTION cries out, '**Hark!***
> *I need an exclamation mark!'*
>
> *Through poetry, we learn how each*
> *Of these make up THE PARTS OF SPEECH.*

We say 'generally considered' because there are also three little words – *the, a* and *an* – and a few others that are categorized as **articles** or **determiners** and you can't really ignore them. We'll come back to them in a minute (p.39), but first let's have a quick look at what parts of speech are all about.

It's just one thing after another

Words from each of the parts of speech are used as **building blocks**: they add to meaning by modifying or qualifying one another. Consider this sentence:

A brown cow in a great, green field ate grass greedily.

By painting a more detailed picture, words limit (modify, qualify – you'll come across all these words to describe the same sort of thing) and thus clarify meaning. In the above sentence, for instance, we are not talking about cows in general; the article *a* tells us we are talking about one specific cow. The cow is not any colour; it is brown. The cow is not just standing there; it is eating grass. Where is it eating grass? In a field. Not any old field; but a great, green one. How is it eating? Greedily.

In fact, that sentence doesn't cover all the parts of speech, so let's add another few words:

A brown cow in a great, green field ate grass greedily, and gosh it grew fat!

The conjunction *and* tells us that we are joining one thought to another. The interjection *gosh* gives us an excuse to write an exclamation mark at the end of the sentence. And *it*, of course, is a pronoun that refers back to the cow.

So let's now look at each of these building blocks in more detail.

DEFINITELY INDEFINITE (OR, ARTICLES)

'A horse, a horse, my kingdom for a horse.'
SHAKESPEARE, *Richard III*

An **article** is any one of a group of things. *I have lost an article of luggage*, for example, means you have lost only one bag of several. In grammar an article is any one of the words *a*, *an* and *the*.

A and *an* are known as **indefinite** articles because they describe nouns in general. *The* restricts the meaning of a noun to make it more specific. Or definite. It is therefore known as the **definite article**.

A drunk man	any old drunk man (he could be anyone – we haven't mentioned him yet)
The drunk man	a specific drunk man (someone we are already talking about)
A drunk man was lurching down the street.	This implies the man is a stranger to all.
The drunk man was crawling down the street.	This implies the speaker/writer or listener/reader already knows something about this man – he has already cropped up.

Bizarrely, however, when speaking in very general terms, *the* can be used instead of *a* to make something less specific:

There was a tiger in my garden.	an individual animal
The tiger is an endangered species.	that is, all of them
I bought a ukulele.	one specific instrument
I play the ukulele.	I can pick up any ukulele and strum away happily on it

---

👋 **Smart Alec:** *The* is the most common word in the English language.

Absolute zero

Another way to make a statement more general is to use no article at all. This is sometimes referred to as the **zero article** and usually applies to plurals or mass nouns (see p.47).

Women are not good with maps.
Shorts are not suitable office attire.
Cats are thankless creatures.
Grammar is hard to learn.

No need for introductions...

Pronouns and proper nouns do not require articles. They stand by themselves.

I am not good at grammar.
David Beckham is better at grammar than I am.

A or *an*?

Rule: nouns or adjectives beginning in a vowel usually take the article *an*, while nouns or adjectives beginning with a consonant take the article *a*.

> **For example:**
> *an orange, a peach*
> *an octopus, a squid*
> *an axe, a chopper*
> *an island, a continent*
> *an orange orange, a red apple*

However, as usual there are exceptions to the rule, because some vowels are sometimes pronounced as if they were consonants, and some *h*s aren't pronounced at all:

> *a unique event,* **an unusual** *event*
> *a horrid man,* **an honourable** *gentleman*
> *an hour,* **an hour** *and* **a half.**
> *a European,* **an Eskimo**
> *a eulogy,* **an epigram**
> *a football match,* **an FA Cup final**

We say *a* unique event because we pronounce the letter *u* in unique as a hard *y* sound – *yoonique.* We pronounce the *h* in *horrid,* but not in *honourable.* We say the *f* sound in *football,* but we pronounce *FA* as *eff A.*

Similarly, abbreviations such as *MP* or *SAS* – pronounced respectively *em pea* and *ess a ess,* sound as if they begin with vowels, and so we say *she is an MP, he is an SAS man.*

☛ **See Me After Class:** There is no *h* at the beginning of the word *aitch.*

An historical note

> 'He was sojourning at an hotel in Bond Street.'
> **ANTHONY TROLLOPE**

Here's a hypothesis – or rather four separate but vaguely related hypotheses – on words beginning with *h* and an unstressed syllable (or why some people say *an history, an hotel* and *an hypothesis*):

1. Once upon a time all educated people spoke French and so pronounced *history*, such as the French word *histoire*, with a silent *h*. Appropriately they gave it the article *an*.

2. Some – less well-educated and therefore non-French-speaking – people spoke badly, were lazy about pronouncing their *aitches*, and so got into the habit of saying *an 'istory*.

3. Educated people disliked dropping aitches, so began to pronounce them in French words that traditionally used the article *an*: *an history*.

4. People spoke too quickly, running together the words *a* and *history*, so that it became pronounced *anistory*. When they paused for breath, and separated things out a bit, they thought the word must be *an history*.

Note the inherent snobbishness of these hypotheses. It crops up a lot in the study of language.

But whatever the origins of the practice may be, the rule is: if the *h* is pronounced (as in *history*, *hotel* and *hypothesis*), the correct article is *a*; if it is not pronounced (as in *honour* and *hour*), use *an*.

☛ **Swot's Corner:** Some of those old grammarians who decreed that *an* should be used before an *h* did so because we aspirated less in those days. Aspiration is the release of air that comes out of our mouths when we speak. If you try talking to a candle flame, you should notice that the flame definitely flickers when you say *hotel* or *history* (aspirated), but much less so when you say *'otel* or *'istory* (unaspirated).

On the other hand, if you try talking to a candle flame, people may think you are just a tiny bit sad.

DEMONSTRATE YOUR DETERMINATION (OR, DETERMINERS)

In fact articles are a subdivision of a class of words called **determiners**, which includes **quantifiers**, **demonstratives** and what in traditional grammar are often called **possessive adjectives** (note that these are also confusingly sometimes called **possessive pronouns**, and we'll meet them again on page 66).

Possessive adjectives – *my, his, her, its, our, your, their* – perform the useful task of telling us what belongs to, or is related to, something else.

*The captain stood firm at the bow of **his** ship as **its** deck was consumed in flames.*
*The bemused sailors redoubled **their** efforts and extinguished the blaze without **his** assistance.*

Used carelessly, however, they can cause confusion:

Both the fashion editors liked her new hat. (Whose hat? If you mean that each fashion editor had a new hat that she liked, try, *Each of the fashion editors liked her new hat*, and if you mean there was only one new hat, be specific: *Both the fashion editors liked Susannah's new hat.*)

Mrs Jones and Mrs Brown disliked their neighbours. (Whose

neighbours? Did Mrs Jones and Mrs Brown cohabit and dislike the same neighbours? Or did each woman dislike her own neighbours? Or possibly her own neighbours and the other woman's neighbours, too?)

Demonstratives are the words *this/that, these/those* (which may also be demonstrative pronouns, see p.67). When used as determiners, they precede the noun in much the same way as *the* or *a*, but are used to differentiate between things that are near at hand (*this, these*) and things that are farther away (*that, those*). The nearness or farness may refer to time or space:

*Does my bum look big in **this** dress* (the one I have on)?
*Ah, do you remember **that** weekend in Paris* (back in the day)?

*I have never seen **these** people before* (though they are standing in front of me now).
*Oh bother, if I had known **those** chocolates* (the ones I have eaten, so they are now in the past) *had arsenic in them, I would have left them alone.*

Quantifiers are words such as *no, either, neither, any, both, few, little, half,* etc. Again, some of these words (or groups of words) may serve as other parts of speech (*either* or *neither* as a conjunction, for example, see p.103, or *little* as an adjective, see p.90), but in this context they go before the noun and tell us the number or, well, quantity of something:

***Neither** councillor has **any** charisma.*
***Every one of the** candidates is a crook.*
*It would be completely hypocritical of me to vote for **any of** that lot.*
***Half the** problems of modern life can be blamed on people like that.*

*There is **little** chance of anyone decent getting in.*
*Do you think these examples are turning into **a bit of a** rant?*

WHAT'S IN A NAME?
(OR, NOUNS)

There are various categories of **noun**, but they are all 'naming words'. They just name different types of thing.

Common noun: a word used to name a person, animal, place, thing or abstract idea, such as *book, smell, dog, parsnip, leg, delight, boredom, success* and *failure*.

Common nouns can be further subdivided into:
Concrete noun: used to name something you can identify with one or more of the five senses, e.g. *parsnip, smell.*
Abstract noun: names something that has no physical existence, e.g. *delight, failure.*

Proper noun: used to name a specific person, animal, place or thing. It is usually written with a capital letter to show its importance, such as *Queen Victoria, Statue of Liberty, Monday, Christmas, Ibiza, Rolls-Royce* and *Noel Edmonds.**

Compound noun: a noun made up of more than one word, usually (but not always) two nouns or a noun and an adjective, to make something with a meaning of its own, such as *apple tree, lion tamer, feel-good factor, tan line, lawsuit, science-fiction* (or indeed *science-fiction writer*) and *will-o'-the-wisp.*

---

* If you've been paying attention, you should already know about capitalizing this sort of word. If not, go back to p.33 and start again.

Wikipedia says that English has a habit of 'creating compounds by concatenating words without case markers', which is a wonderfully nonsensical way of saying that we just bung words together to make other words or phrases: thus a *science-fiction writer* is a *writer* who writes *fiction* based on *science*, but there is nothing in the form of the words to tell us whether they are adjectives or nouns or whatever. And as you can see, these compounds may end up as a single word, two or more separate words or two or more words with one or more hyphens. But let's not get into hyphens just yet...*

The numbers game

Another way of categorizing nouns is to divide them into **countable** and **mass** (or **non-countable**) nouns.

Countable nouns are (reasonably enough) used to name something that can be counted, such as *one plate, two eggs, three sausages*. It's countable if you can ask *how many are there?* or state *there are a number of men/chairs/staplers* – because you can easily count the specific number of items.†

A **mass** or **non-countable noun** refers to something that cannot reasonably be counted and therefore has no plural, such as *air, art, milk, money, stupidity, sand* and *wisdom*. Quantities of non-countable nouns are described as *an amount of hair/sand/rubbish*, either because they refer to an unspecified *amount* of stuff or because there are too many individual bits (e.g. of hair or sand) to number. We can't ask *how many?* with non-countable nouns (how many milk, how many traffic); it's simply *how much?*

---

* But if you *do* want to get into hyphens just yet, see p.165.
† Or should it be *there is a number of men?* Turn to p.135.

Five items or less (less what?)

A common mistake is the confusion of *less* and *fewer*. Supermarkets almost always get it wrong.

Use *fewer* with countable nouns, e.g. *five items or fewer*.

Use *less* with non-countable nouns, e.g. *less traffic than yesterday*.

We're all in it together

A **collective noun** is one that refers to a group or number of individuals; common examples include *audience, class, family, flock, group, jury, orchestra, parliament, staff* and *team*, and there are many more.

Strictly speaking all these words are singular and take a singular verb. Straightforward enough, you might think. The problem is that a collective noun can refer to a whole group acting as a single entity and also to all the members of that group, acting as individuals.

Are you still there?

Rule: We use a singular verb with a collective noun when we mean the whole group acting as one; we use the plural verb when we are referring to the actions of the individuals within the group. For example:

The battalion lost all its men in that battle.　　All the men died in the battle.

The battalion lost their lives in that battle.　　All the men died, but not necessarily all at once.

The group was waylaid by the airport bar.	All members of the group went to the bar.
The group took so long drinking their cocktails that they nearly missed their flight.	But they did not all drink the same cocktail at the same time.
The staff has gone crazy.	All employees are acting strangely.
The staff have locked themselves into their offices.	But they are not all locked in the same office.

Some people call this **formal agreement** – when you say *the staff is...* – and **notional agreement** – *the [members of the] team are.**

A related source of confusion lies in the names of sports teams. *Manchester United*, for example, is not a collective noun. It's a proper noun (hence the capital letters – see p.33) and it should strictly speaking – those words again – be treated as singular. So, bizarrely, should *Glasgow Rangers*, *Bristol Rovers* and the *Boston Red Sox*. On the other hand, there is no denying that lots of people say *Manchester United **are** in the final* and frankly only the most pedantic among us (and Chelsea supporters) are likely to be offended.

---

* We found these terms on a website under the heading 'Metonymic merging of grammatical number', so it is probably safe to say you needn't worry too much about them.

☛ **Swot's Corner:** To avoid confusion with collective nouns, it is often sensible to reword a sentence. Try *The hotel manager is offering members of the wedding party a discount on their rooms* instead of *The hotel is/are offering the wedding party a discount on its/their rooms.*

Adjectives treated as collective nouns – *the rich, the homeless, the lonely* – are always plural and require a plural verb, e.g. *the rich are getting richer.*

I'm the leader of the pack/smack/shiver

There are scores of collective nouns to describe parts of the animal (and particularly bird) kingdom. Some of them are genuinely useful (a flock of sheep and a herd of elephants, for example, if sheep and elephants crop up in your conversation to any great extent). Others are obscure or just plain silly, but here is a small sample of them:

a shrewdness of apes
a wake of buzzards
an intrusion of cockroaches
a pod of dolphins
a business of ferrets
a tower of giraffes
a bloat of hippopotamuses
a smack of jellyfish
a troop of kangaroos
a labour of moles
a parliament of owls
a bevy of quail

> *an unkindness of ravens*
> *a shiver of sharks*
> *a streak of tigers*
> *a descent of woodpeckers*

Is it common or proper?

Lots of words have come into English because of the man (with the honourable exception of Mrs Amelia Bloomer, it is usually a man) who invented or popularized the item concerned. At some stage in the evolution of all these words, they would have been proper nouns, and thus spelt with a capital, but as the word became more commonplace and the association with a person was forgotten, the capital tended to be abandoned, too.

The only two of this list that merit a capital in the dictionaries are those whose inventors lived into the twentieth century. We give them ten years.

Biro   László József Bíró (1899–1985), Hungarian inventor of the ballpoint pen.

boycott   Captain Charles C. Boycott, Irish land agent ostracized by his neighbours in 1880.

cardigan   The 7th Earl of Cardigan (1797–1868), after whom the garment is named. He was clearly a fashion icon of his day.

dunce The blessed John Duns Scotus (died 1308), one of the most important theologians and philosophers of the Middle Ages, later accused of unsound reasoning. And presumably made to stand in a corner wearing a pointy hat.

Hoover W. H. 'Boss' Hoover (1849–1932). American businessman who first patented (but did not invent) the vacuum cleaner named after him.

leotard Jules Léotard, nineteenth-century French acrobat after whom the garment is named.

lynch mob Captain William Lynch (1742–1820), Virginia justice of the peace at the time of the American Revolution; had a fondness for summarily executing people with whom he disagreed.

mac Charles Macintosh (1766–1843), Scottish chemist who patented a coat made from rubberized material.

mausoleum King Mausolos of Caria (died 353 BC), whose tomb was one of the Seven Wonders of the Ancient World.

shrapnel Major-General Henry Shrapnel (1761–1842), English artillery officer, who designed a new type of artillery shell.

silhouette   Etienne de Silhouette (1709–67), unpopular
finance minister of Louis XV who imposed
harsh economic demands upon the French
people. His name became associated with
anything done cheaply – particularly the
simple form of portraiture that became
popular at the time and enabled people to
joke that the finance minister was saving
money on coloured paints as well as
everything else. We haven't had a
Chancellor of the Exchequer who was half
as funny in years.

ONE DIE, TWO DICE (OR, SINGULAR AND PLURAL)

'We want people owning their home – we want people
owning a businesses.'
GEORGE W. BUSH, 18 APRIL 2008

When a noun means only one thing it is **singular**. When it is
more than one it is **plural**. The rules on how to make a plural start
off straightforwardly, but then do tend to head out into left field.
Hang in there.

1.   Most singular nouns are made plural by adding the
letter *s: book, bell, candle = books, bells, candles.*

2. However, if you add an *s* to such nouns as *church, bus, fox, bush, bench, Jones* and *waltz*, they become difficult to pronounce. Which is why we add *-es* and create an extra syllable: *churches, buses, Joneses...*

3. If a noun ends in *y*, and the letter before the *y* is a vowel, again just add an *s*: *key* = *keys*. However, if a noun ends in *y* and the letter before the *y* is a consonant, the *y* must be changed to an *i* and followed by *es*: *lady* = *ladies/ gallery* = *galleries.* That's sorted then.

No, wait, there's an exception: This rule does not apply to proper nouns: *one penny, several pennies,* but *Mr and Mrs Penny* become *the Pennys.*

4. To form the plurals of nouns ending in *ff*, add that *s*: *cliffs, toffs* etc. However, words ending in a single *f* or in *fe* need to have these letters replaced with a *v* – oh, and then add *es*: *leaf* = *leaves, wife* = *wives.* Got that? Good, because there are exceptions.

> **Exceptions to rule 4:**
> *Dwarfs and chiefs*
> *Will cause you griefs.*
> *As will proofs, roofs, safes, beliefs.*
> *Hooves and hoofs can either be,*
> *So too, scarfs and scarves, you see.*
> *To wharfs and wharves, you may refer,*
> *And turfs and turves, as you prefer.*

And just when you thought you were getting the hang of it, humans have one *life*, cats have nine *lives*, but artists can paint as many still *lifes* as they like.

5. Many words ending in *o* can be made plural by adding -*s*: *zoos, kangaroos, igloos, solos, sopranos, discos, photos, Eskimos, infernos.* Others – seemingly chosen at random – need -*es*: **Buffaloes** *have trampled my* **potatoes** *and* **tomatoes**. *If we sit outside to play* **dominoes** *we shall be plagued by* **mosquitoes**.

6. A number of nouns have irregular plurals, which is why we do not say *Are you mans or mouses?*, and why the plural of *house* is *houses*, but the plural of *louse* is *lice*.* Then there's *goose/geese, tooth/teeth, child/ children, ox/oxen* (but not *box/boxen*).

🐦 **Swot's Corner:** The plural of *talisman* is not *talismen* but *talismans*. Why? Because its origins have nothing to do with *man* or *men*. The word comes to us from Arabic and medieval Greek via French or Spanish. But of course you knew that.

Rule: the rules always apply, except when they don't. With irregular forms such as *child/children*, sorry, you just have to learn them.

---

* Marilyn Monroe in *Gentlemen Prefer Blondes* did sing about those *louses* going back to their *spouses*, but she meant a particular sort of louse.

> **Sorry, don't know the plural…**
> *Dear Sir,*
> *Please send me a mongoose.*
> *Oh, by the way, send me another one, too.*

In big-game hunting it appears to be fair game to dispense with the usual plurals. Hence we might shoot *several gazelle, two leopard, three lion, three elephant* and *six wild pig*. This has a slightly old-fashioned feel and does somehow suggest that you are going out to kill the poor beasts and hang their heads on your wall.

And on the agendum today

Some nouns have no (or a rarely used) singular form:

alms	*marginalia*	*tidings*
bellows	*oats*	*tongs*
billiards	*pants*	*trousers*
braces	*pliers*	*tweezers*
clothes	*scissors*	*vespers*
dregs	*shorts*	*victuals*
eaves	*thanks*	*vittles*

NB Nouns such as these require a **measure word**, for example *a pair* of trousers, *some* thanks. You cannot say *one scissors*. Nor, happily, can you sow *just the one wild oat*.

Singularity is almost invariably a clue

No, it isn't. That was just Sherlock Holmes being a smartarse. With some nouns, singularity is more trouble than it's worth.

Such nouns have a plural form but do what the dictionaries describe as 'functioning as a singular'. Others can function as either a singular or a plural. Which is, frankly, no help at all to those of us who like rules. Still others function as a singular in some senses and as a plural in others.

Yikes.

Well, if the rules don't help, let's try a few examples.

*Mumps **is** nasty, measles **is** measly* is perfectly correct. But so too is *mumps **are** nasty, measles **are** measly.*

Sports with a plural form tend to take a singular verb when we mean them generically, but a plural when we mean something more countable, such as *exercises.* So:

*Athletics **is** tiresome.*   meaning the whole concept

*Gymnastics **are** a great way to*   meaning gymnastic exercises
start the day.

Pilates, by the way, is the name of the man who invented it, so it is singular. And harder than it looks.

A similar distinction can be made with academic subjects.

Acoustics is singular when we mean the study of sound, but plural when we mean sound qualities: *the acoustics **were** dreadful.* Similarly, if you study *ethics* or *politics*, it is a singular subject, but if you bring a person's *ethics* into question or complain about company *politics*, they are plural.

One sheep, two sheep...

The following nouns take the same form whether they are singular or plural. So what would Sherlock Holmes have to say about that?

aircraft	*kudos*	*series*
cannon	*means*	*shambles*
deer	*offspring*	*sheep*
haddock	*premises**	*species†*
		trout

Take your pick...

All self-respecting pedants know about **Latin plurals**; a smattering (and rapidly diminishing number) of older ones know about Greek, too. But here a little learning can be a dangerous thing, because it is easy to assume that a word ending in *-us* is Latin second declension, and therefore has a plural ending in *-i*: *abaci, cacti, incubi, succubi.* Then along comes a word such as *platypus*, whose origins are Greek and whose plural is strictly speaking *platypuses*, to catch you out just when you thought you were being clever.

---

* In the sense of 'escorting someone off the premises'; the singular form means a supposition.

† The little used *specie*, meaning money in coins as opposed to paper or bullion, is not actually a singular of *species* and comes from a different root altogether.

A number of words ending in -*on* are derived from Greek neuter nouns and have a plural form ending in -*a*: *criterion/criteria*, *phenomenon/phenomena* etc.

Some words ending in -*is* are Latin third declension in origin and have a plural form -*es*: *crisis/crises*, *thesis/theses* (pronounced -*eeze* as in *cheese* or *sneeze*).

And then there are those that have decided to ignore their classical background altogether and allow us to choose between two (or even more) plural forms, some of them rather suspect:

hippopotamus	hippopotamuses, hippopotami
octopus	octopi, octopodes, octopuses
oxymoron	oxymorons, oxymora
necropolis	necropolises, necropoles, necropoleis, necropoli
rhinoceros	rhinoceroses, rhinoceros, rhinoceri, rhinocerotes
syllabus	syllabuses, syllabi
terminus	termini, terminuses
uterus	uteri, uteruses

☛ **Swot's Corner:** *Octopus* is a one-word minefield, because it is a Latinized form of a Greek word, *oktopous*, whose 'correct' plural form would be *octopodes*. *Chambers Dictionary* describes that as archaic and gives *octopuses* as the correct form. '*Octopi*,' it says austerely, 'is wrong.' But right or wrong, if enough people use it, *octopi*, which has no justification in etymological terms, will work its way into the dictionaries in time.

Keeping up with the Joneses

When we talk about a family in the plural, we need to add an *s* to the **family name**, e.g. *the Smiths, the Windsors.* However, if the family name ends in *s, x, ch, sh,* or *z*, we add *-es*: *the Joneses, the Foxes, the Bushes* etc. Same rules as *churches* and *waltzes*, see p.54.

☛ **See Me After Class:** *The Venables's came to our house this weekend.*
Do not make a family name plural by using an apostrophe.

Exceptions: When a name ends in an *s* with a hard *z* sound, we don't add any ending to form the plural. *We have the Morrises and the Richards coming to lunch.* It is equally acceptable to say *The Misses Brown are coming to tea*, or *The Miss Browns are coming to tea.*

Compounding the problem

The rule with **plural compound nouns** is to pluralize the base element of the compound noun – that is, generally, the most important element of the word or phrase:

*We've got our **mother-in-laws** staying so we've nipped out for a pint* is wrong;
Mothers-in-law *and* **daughters-in-law** *don't always get along* is right,

because the key element of the phrase is *mother* (or *daughter*). Ask yourself *What sort of mother? A mother-in-law*. Similarly:

*The role of **Secretary of State** varies between countries, and in some cases there are multiple **Secretaries of State**.*
Doctors Payne and Betterman *were speaking at the conference* (there is more than one doctor, but only one called Payne and only one called Betterman).
*Bertie and Bingo were both idle but amiable **men-about-town**.*

The media is the message

In addition to those mentioned above, here are a few more words whose origins we seem to have forgotten, but in these cases – because the plural forms don't end in *s* – we are beginning to use them as singulars. Lots of perfectly literate people now say (and some even write) *The data **was** incorrect* or *The media **is** very hostile to government policy*, but the purists still cling on to the distinction between singular and plural.

Plural	Singular
bacteria	*bacterium*
dice	*die*

formulae	*formula*
graffiti	*graffito*
candelabra	*candelabrum*
data	*datum*
media	*medium*
opera	*opus*
paparazzi	*paparazzo*

One plural that has lost the fight is *pease*, which used to be the regular plural of *pea*. Now *peas* is found pretty much everywhere except in the phrase *pease pudding* and the nursery rhyme about whether it is hot or cold.

✋ **Smart Alec:** If you add an *s* to the plural words *adventures, bras, cares, cosines, deadlines, millionaires, ogres, princes* and *timelines* they revert to a singular form: *adventuress, brass, caress, cosiness, deadliness, millionairess, ogress, princess* and *timeliness*.

By the way, *genie* and *genius* have the same plural: *genii*.

THOU AND THEE (OR, PRONOUNS)

Going back to our poem (p.37), 'In place of noun the pronoun stands'. So a **pronoun** is used to avoid repeating a noun over and over again. Imagine if you were writing a summary of this book and had to say, *Many people find grammar difficult. Lots of people were never taught grammar at school. Grammar has therefore become a source of anxiety. Indeed, some people might call grammar a minefield.* Just because nobody had thought to invent the words *it* or *them*.

The noun to which a pronoun refers is sometimes called the **antecedent**. So in *Many people find grammar difficult. Lots of them were never taught it at school, people* is the antecedent of *them* and *grammar* is the antecedent of *it*.

> 'The masculine pronouns are he, his and him,
> But imagine the feminine she, shis and shim.'
> **Anon**

There are various categories of pronoun, depending on the function they perform in a sentence.

The **subject pronouns** are *I, you, he, she, it, we, they* and the equivalent **object pronouns** are *me, you, him, her, it, us, them.* If we've lost you here, see p.126 for an explanation of subject and object. But it boils down to the difference between *I love him* and *He loves me*, which could be quite significant.

✍ **Smart Alec:** Since *pronoun* is a noun, why isn't *proverb* a verb?

A bit about SEX

Ahem. The English language does not have a **singular pronoun** that encapsulates both genders. It used to be that 'the masculine was deemed to embrace the feminine', but 1960s feminism put a stop to that sort of hanky-panky and has left us with a grammatical problem ever since. Some people meticulously write *he or she, his or hers*, wherever it crops up, but this quickly becomes cumbersome and tedious. Others go for *s/he*, but that still leaves them with the his/her dilemma. Still others go to the opposite extreme and use *she* or *her* throughout (so the feminine is now embracing the masculine, as it were).

Lots of people nowadays fudge this by using *their* as a non-gender-specific singular, as in *the judge* (who may be a man or a woman, we don't know and it would be sexist to assume either) *adjusted their wig*. It isn't pretty, but sometimes being purist is no oil painting either.

It's all relative

The **relative pronouns** are *who, what, whom, that, whose* and *which* and their role is to introduce subordinate clauses that tell us more about the noun that precedes them. For example:

*The waiter **who** served you may remember what time you left.*
*The cakes **that** I baked for the children do not have any nuts in them.*
*The boy **whose** name was Sue made a lot of money out of a song bemoaning the fact **that** his name was Sue.*
*He **whom** the gods love dies young.*

Which can also be used to refer back to an entire clause: *The sun was shining over Glastonbury,* **which** *didn't seem right at all.*

Excellent reflexes

> 'And not in me: I am myself alone.'
> **SHAKESPEARE,** *Henry VI*

Reflexive pronouns are formed by adding *self* or *selves* to the basic pronoun: *myself, oneself, yourself, himself, herself, itself, ourselves, yourselves, themselves.* They are used when the subject and object of a verb are the same person or thing:

I can look after **myself***.*
Speak for **yourself***!*
We enjoyed **ourselves** *immensely.*
The kids can never be trusted to behave **themselves** *when the babysitter is there.*

They can also be used to avoid ambiguity. Compare these sentences:

Tom had done surprisingly well in his exams. The teacher was very pleased with **him** (i.e. pleased with Tom).
Tom had done surprisingly well in his exams. The teacher was very pleased with **himself** (i.e. the teacher was pleased with the teacher).

These pronouns can also be used for emphasis, or to mean 'alone, unaided': *I can't see what anyone sees in* Big Brother, **myself***.* Or: *Did you really do all the decorating* **yourself***?*

Over-use of reflexive pronouns in this emphatic sense is one of the banes of modern speech. *I think* is just as persuasive as *I myself think*, and (we're sorry to be dogmatic, but please bear with us this once) that common piece of modern estate-agentese, *It's ideal for yourselves* is just plain wrong.

> 'Every one to rest themselves betake.'
> **SHAKESPEARE,** *The Rape of Lucrece*

Let's reciprocate

The **reciprocal pronouns** are *each other* and *one another*. *Each other* refers to two people or things; *one another* to more than two.

*The two candidates who were still in contention congratulated **each other**. The others adjourned to the bar to commiserate with **one another**.*

What's mine is yours

The **possessive pronouns** are *my, mine, your(s), his, her(s), our(s), their(s)* and *its* (and note that they never – repeat never – need an apostrophe: see p.175 for some common confusions). *Mine, yours, his, hers, ours, theirs* and *its* tend to be used after the noun to which they refer and mean 'the thing belonging to or associated with me/you/whoever':

*He had forgotten his gloves again, so I gave him **mine**.*
*Put that book back where you found it: it isn't **yours**.*
*We were madly envious because their house was much nicer than **ours**.*

I don't want to be specific...

There are a number of useful pronouns that we can use when we don't want, or are unable, to specify exactly what we are talking about: *all, another, any, anyone, anything, each, everybody, everyone, everything, few, many, no one, nobody, none, nothing, one, several, some, somebody, someone.* These are called **indefinite pronouns**.

*I think **someone** is in the house.*
*You've eaten most of the chocolates: there are only **a few** left.*
*In space, **no one** can hear you scream.*

By the way, there is no difference in grammatical terms between *no one* and *nobody, someone* and *somebody, anyone* and *anybody*: for once you can just use whichever you like.

Talking of this and that

The **demonstrative pronouns** are *this, that, these* and *those* – the same words as the demonstrative determiners we met earlier, but used in a slightly different way.

*Please take **this** home with you and study it.*	meaning, perhaps, **this** book
*Take **that** to the cleaners, will you.*	**that** jacket
*I want **these** removed at once.*	**these** dirty dishes
***Those** are no good to anybody.*	**those** old clothes

Let's investigate…

Interrogative pronouns take the place of a noun in a question.

Who *is that?*	The answer might be: That is Homer Simpson.
What *is that?*	That is a picture of Homer Simpson.
Which *is that?*	Which of the many pictures of Homer Simpson in the world are you talking about?
To whom *should I give the doughnuts?*	Pretty obvious, really.

Some common confusions

Their/Theirs/There/There's/They're

Their is a possessive pronoun, showing ownership. *It was **their** version of the story that was reported on the news.*

Theirs is also a possessive pronoun indicating that something belongs to more than one person. *That version of the story is **theirs.***

There is an adverb that indicates a place or position. *My new car is over **there**. **There** is a monkey in that tree.*

There's means *there is*. ***There's** that ring you were looking for.*

They're means *they are*. ***They're** a very happy couple even though they fight all the time.*

Its/It's

Its is a possessive pronoun. *We thought the cat was lost, but it somehow found **its** way home.*

It's means *it is*. ***It's** not fair.*

Whose/Who's

Whose is a possessive pronoun. *The boy **whose** trousers were flown from the flagpole.*

Whose can also be an interrogative pronoun. ***Whose** trousers are those?*

Who's means *who is*. *The boy **who's** being told off for putting them there.*

Who, which or that?

Rule: Use *who* to refer to people.
Use *which* to refer to animals or inanimate objects.
Use *that* as a less formal substitute for either.

*The people **who** matter will be impressed by this. (The people **that** matter is not incorrect, but is less formal.)*
*The tigers **which** (or **that**) come from Siberia have thick fur to protect them against the cold.*
*The house **which** (or **that**) we used to live in has been knocked down to make way for a supermarket.*
*The song **which** (or **that**) he wrote never made it into the charts.*

In the last two examples, the antecedent is the object of the following clause (we used to live in the house, he wrote the song). In these cases, another option is to omit the relative pronoun altogether:

The house we used to live in…
The song he wrote…

And, on the subject of which and that, don't miss the exciting instalment on restrictive and non-restrictive clauses later in the book (see p.139).

WHAT A TO-DO (OR, VERBS)

✍ **Smart Alec:** When somebody greets us with *How do you do?* why don't we ever reply *Do what??*

A **verb** is a 'doing word': *I do, you go, he runs, we sleep, they sneeze*. A verb also expresses a state of being: *I am, it is, we live*. Verbs have a lot of clout. They make things happen.

I books
You grammar
We money

mean nothing without a verb.

I write books
You learn grammar
We earn money

make perfect sense. And are good things. Particularly the last one.

To be or not to be

With verbs, we start with the **infinitive**, which is made up of the preposition *to* and the basic form of the verb:

To be, or not to be, that is the question.
To sleep, perchance to dream.
To have and to hold.

These verbs have meaning – we know what *to be, to sleep, to dream, to have, to hold* mean – but they don't tell us anything specific about the action that is being performed, the time it is (or was or will be or may have been) being done, or the number of people doing it. For that, we need either:

to **conjugate** the verb – that is, change the ending to show a change of meaning (*he guffaws, I guffawed*); or
to add an **auxiliary** or helping verb to specify time and number (*I*

will *guffaw, you* **are** *guffawing, he* **has** *guffawed*).

Once you have conjugated a verb and added any auxiliaries you want to make the action complete, you have a **finite verb**. (As in, not an infinitive, you see? Clever, eh?)

To boldly split

> But surely, this is a practice entirely unknown to English speakers and writers. It seems to me that we ever regard the *to* of the infinitive as inseparable from its verb. And, when we have already a choice between two forms of expression, *scientifically to illustrate* and *to illustrate scientifically*, there seems no good reason for flying in the face of common usage.
>
> HENRY ALFORD, *Plea for the Queen's English,* **1864**

The old rule was simple: *never split an infinitive* – that is, on pain of death, never put a word between the *to* and the rest of the verb. The example everyone trundles out at this point is *Star Trek*'s 'To boldly go…'

It is, however, probably one of the dafter rules to come out of the old grammarians' insistence on applying Latin rules to English: Latin infinitives are one word – *amare, potare, studere* – so couldn't be split anyway. Modern scholars reckon that splitting an infinitive is perfectly acceptable if the alternative would be clumsy or ambiguous. In the following sentences, for example, we think that the non-split version is more elegant and the meaning is equally clear, so it is preferable. But it is surely preferable *because it is more elegant,* not because the infinitive is unsplit.

*Many people choose **to incorrectly split** an infinitive in everyday speech.* ☒
*Many people **incorrectly choose to split** an infinitive in everyday speech.* ☑

*They decided **to quickly devour** the pie.* ☒
*They decided **to devour the pie quickly**.* ☑

*She put aside extra time **to closely mark** the exam papers.* ☒
*She put aside extra time **to mark the exam papers closely**.* ☑

On the other hand, this fragment (from a *Daily Telegraph* report) scrupulously avoids splitting the infinitive and in so doing sacrifices clarity: *A family doctor who installed a camera **secretly to film** a woman using his bathroom...* What was it that was done secretly? The installation or the filming? (Or, given the context, perhaps both?)

'The English-speaking world may be divided into (1) those who neither know nor care what a split infinitive is; (2) those who do not know, but care very much; (3) those who know and condemn; (4) those who know and approve; (5) those who know and distinguish... Those who neither know nor care are the vast majority, and are a happy folk, to be envied by most of the minority classes.'

H. W. FOWLER, *Modern English Usage,* **1926**

A few irregularities

Regular verbs – those that follow the rules – are conjugated as follows:

Present tense:	*I love, you love, he loves, we love, they love*
Past tense:	*I loved, you loved, he loved, we loved, they loved*
Present participle*:	*loving, biting.*

(Note that if a verb ends in *e*, we drop the *e* to form the present participle. If not, we just add *-ing*: *wanting, hanging, staggering,* etc.).

Because this is English, however, there are, inevitably, lots of **irregular verbs**. Some past tenses and past participles are formed by adding *-t* instead of *-ed* (see below). Then we have *to drink,* which becomes *I drank, you drank,* etc. in the past tense, whereas *to think* becomes *I thought. To speak* becomes *I spoke,* but *to squeak* and *to sneak* are regular and become *I squeaked* and *I sneaked.*

The most thoroughly irregular verbs of all are the common ones *to be* and *to go: I am, you are, he is, we are, they are, I was, you were,* for heaven's sake. *To go* is OK in the present tense, but *I went?* What's that all about?

Again, it's the irritating feature of irregular forms that there's no apparent logic to them and you just have to learn them.

---

* We'll come back to what the present participle is all about in a minute.

Lessons learnt (or should that be 'learned'?)

If you are unsure which ending to give to the past tense and past participle of irregular verbs such as *burn, dream, lean, learn,* and *smell,* you may be relieved to know that it is fine to use either a *-t* or an *-ed* ending. Just make sure you go for one or the other, because mixing them looks messy. For the record, British English speakers tend to *have learnt* their lessons, while American English speakers *have learned* theirs.

Back me up, will you?

Auxiliary verbs are used 'to indicate the tense, voice, mood, etc. of another verb where this is not indicated by inflection'. Don't you just love dictionaries? It means they are the little words you stick in the front of verbs. There are twenty-three of them, which can be learnt by singing them to the tune of 'Jingle Bells' – if you really, truly have nothing better to do with your time.

> *may, might, must*
> *be, being, been*
> *am, are*
> *is, was, were*
> *do, does, did*
> *should, could, would*
> *have, had, has*
> *will, can*
> *shall*

So they can express simple things such as *I **am** coming,* slightly more complicated ones such as *it **shall be** done,* or even more complex ones with up to three auxiliaries attached to one main verb: *He **must have been** feeling unhappy for some time.*

Must and *may*, along with *should and ought*, are also called **modal verbs**: they give information about the mood of the verb (see p.83), expressing such things as obligation (*you **must** be home by midnight, he **ought** to pay before leaving the restaurant*), recommendation (*you **should** ring and apologize*) or possibility (*I **may** do as you ask, but then again I **may** not*).

May or might? Can or could?

Strictly speaking, *may* and *can* operate in the present tense, *might* and *could* in the past or in the conditional (see p.82).

***Can** you lend me a tenner?*	Do you have the money?
***Could** you lend me a tenner?*	Would you be so very kind as to entrust me with this sum, secure in the knowledge that I shall pay it back in the fullness of time?

However, this is another distinction that is beginning to be lost in modern-day speech and writing.

Can/could also indicate *capability* or *possibility*, whereas *may/might* grant us *permission* to do something.

***Can** I drive your Rolls-Royce?*	Well, yes, if your feet can reach the pedals and you understand the concept of a steering wheel.
***May** I drive your Rolls-Royce?*	Over my dead body.

Most people in the English-speaking world seem to have had a schoolteacher who, in response to the question *Can I go to the loo?*, would raise an eyebrow and say, *I don't know – **can** you?*

☞ See Me After Class

Could have/could of

There is no verb *to of. He could've told me* is a short form of

*He could **have** told me.*

Try and/try to

Try and is wrong. *Try to* get it right.

About whom are we talking?

For the purposes of grammar, there are only three **persons** (not people, there are loads of them) in the world:

first person: the speaker (*I, me, we, us*)
second person: the hearer (*you*)
third person: the person or thing spoken of (*he, she, it, they, him, her, them*)

In modern English, *you* serves as both singular and plural, but always takes a plural verb – *you are my lucky star*, *you were made for me*, *you drive me crazy* – even when only one person is being addressed. *Thou* and *thee* were once the singular forms, but they are now never used except as deliberate archaisms, in church and in some dialects.

✋ **Smart Alec:** Many languages have both informal and formal words for *you*: the French *tu* and *vous* and the German *Du* and *Sie*, for example. English only has *you*, having done away with *thou* centuries ago. But did you know that *thou* was in fact the more informal of the two? English has preserved the impeccably polite word rather than the chummy one. Now why should that be?

The voice of reason

And there are two voices: **active** and **passive**.

Rule: with the active voice the subject acts; with the passive voice the subject is acted upon.

Active: *The teacher reprimanded the boy* because *he spilt ink on his copybook.*
Passive: *The boy was reprimanded* because *ink was spilt on his copybook.*

The two sentences say the same thing but with different emphasis. Using the passive voice too often can make writing dull (let's get on with some action!). However, consider:

If it were done when 'tis done then 'twere well it were

done quickly.

*Should auld acquaintance **be forgot**, and never **brought to mind**?*

*Yossarian **was moved** very deeply by the absolute simplicity of this clause of Catch-22.*

*The stars **are not wanted** now.*

The passive should not be ruled out altogether. It may be found to have its uses.

> 'C-l-e-a-n, *clean*, verb active, to make bright, to scour.
> W-i-n, *win*, d-e-r, *der*, *winder*, a casement. When the
> boy knows this out of the book, he goes and does it.'
> **CHARLES DICKENS,** *Nicholas Nickleby*

It's raining pronouns

In English – and certainly in British English – we use a little-known thing called the **weather verb** an awful lot.

It is raining.
It is freezing.
It is in the nineties.

What is this nameless, shapeless *it* that is doing all these things? Well, it is known simply as the **dummy subject**, a handy little word that enables us to get to the part we all love: describing the weather. Without it we'd be going around saying *The sky is raining, the sun is hot*, and so on, which might – perish the thought – make talking about the weather boring.

Getting tense

> 'They said: "You're Laurie Lee, aren't you? Well, just you sit there for the present." I sat there all day but I never got it. I ain't going back there again.'
> **LAURIE LEE**, *Cider With Rosie*

Tenses add time to verbs. They put actions into the past, present and future, the may-yet-be or the might-have-been.

*I **do** ballet on Tuesdays.*	I do this habitually, and will continue to do this.
*I **am doing** ballet at the moment.*	I am doing this either right at this moment – so I can't come to the phone – or over a longer but current period of time: perhaps I used to do salsa but have changed.
*I **have done** ballet for years.*	I did ballet in the past and up to and including the present, but I may be getting bored with it now.
*I **have been doing** ballet for years.*	I did ballet in the past and have continued it until the present time and probably will continue in the future. I haven't finished with it yet. Ballet is here for the duration.

*I **did do** ballet once upon a time.*	I did ballet at some indefinite time in the past. It belongs there. I have given it up in the present.
*I **used to do** ballet, but now I do jazz.*	I no longer do ballet.
*I **was doing** ballet on Tuesdays, but now they've changed it to Fridays.*	I was doing ballet on Tuesdays until recently. I may or may not be doing it on Fridays.
*I **would do** ballet if they hadn't changed the class to a Friday.*	If it could be changed to suit me, I would consider doing ballet in the future.
*I **had done** ballet for years, before I changed to jazz.*	I had given up ballet before I took up jazz. There is nothing to suggest whether or not I am still doing jazz.
*I **had been doing** ballet for years before anyone told me I had a crooked spine.*	I was still doing ballet – the action was ongoing – at some time in the past when something else happened.
*I **shall do** ballet again one day.*	I intend to/predict that I shall do ballet in the future.
*I **shall have done** my ballet exam by the time we go on holiday.*	A future action will be completed by or before a specified time in the future.

*I **shall be doing** the ballet performance on Saturday.*

It is definitely going to happen at this specific point in the future.

Exactly how many tenses there are in English is arguable. Some grammarians claim that there are only two: the present and the past. (Presumably they let the future take care of itself.) Some say the traditional number is twelve, though others have described as many as thirty and, just to confuse us, some tenses have more than one name. But here are fourteen that should get you through most situations (or ballet positions).

present simple	*I pirouette*
present continuous	*I am pirouetting*
present perfect	*I have pirouetted*
present perfect continuous	*I have been pirouetting*
past simple (also known as **preterite**)	*I did pirouette, I pirouetted*
imperfect	*I used to pirouette*
past continuous	*I was pirouetting*
conditional	*I would pirouette*
pluperfect/past perfect	*I had pirouetted*
past perfect continuous	*I had been pirouetting*
future	*I will pirouette*

future perfect	*I will have pirouetted*
future continuous	*I will be pirouetting*
future perfect continuous	*I will have been pirouetting*

Famous last words

'I am about to – or I am going to – die. Either expression is correct.'

FRENCH GRAMMARIAN DOMINIQUE BOUHOURS, WHO DIED IN 1702

Back to the future

In the **future tense**, *shall* refers to the first person, *will* to the second and third. So: *I **shall** be at home tonight. **Will** you come round?*

But if you want to be emphatic, reverse the trend:

*I **will** be ready on time, I promise.*
*I don't care what your wicked stepmother says: you **shall** go to the ball.*

*I **shall** drown; no one **will** save me!*	I should like to be saved but everyone is ignoring me.
*I **will** drown; no one **shall** save me!*	I am determined to drown; I forbid anyone to throw me a life belt.

Judging by your mood...

Verbs, like the rest of us, act differently depending on which **mood** they are in. There are three moods: **indicative**, **imperative** and **subjunctive**.

The **indicative mood** makes a statement or asks a question:

I'm wet, I'm cold and I'm hungry.
Winter is almost here.
He will come.
Is that the best you can do?

The **imperative mood** gives us a command:

Chill out!
Do as I say!
Don't eat the daisies!
And even the more politely phrased: *Please look after this bear.*

Easy-peasy. Unfortunately the **subjunctive mood** is so complicated that it deserves a subheading of its own.

If only it were that easy

The **subjunctive** sounds scarier than it is, and has a tendency to fill people with horror. Let's start with a couple of examples:

*I wish it **weren't** going to snow again* (but it is).
*If it **were** to snow* (which it may or may not do, we don't know yet), *they would not be able to get home.*

I were or *it were* may sound odd, but they're right when you are using the subjunctive.

Rule: If you know something for a fact use *was*. If something is contrary to fact, or if you are imagining a future or different situation to the one you are in, use *were*.

*When I **was** young* (fact: I *was* young once) *I was taught Latin* (it's true, I *was* taught Latin).

*When he **was** young and handsome* (he *was* young and handsome once) *he was also arrogant.*

*I **was** that man* (you *were* indeed).

When I was poor (I once *was* indeed poor), *I wasn't unhappy.*

but

*If I **were** you* (but I'm not), *I should teach myself Latin.*

*If I **were** to teach you Latin* (supposing that I taught you Latin), *would you study hard?*

*If I **were** to be young and handsome again* (but I can't be, alas), *I wouldn't be so arrogant about it.*

*If I **were** that sort of man* (but I'm not).

*If I **were** rich* (but I might never be rich), *would I be happier than I am now?*

*I wish I **were** taller* (but I am currently stuck at this height).

A number of **set phrases** in English – *come what may, far be it from me, the powers that be* – use the subjunctive, but the joy of set phrases is that you don't have to think about them.

Rattigan (child genius): 'If only that was possible.'
The Doctor: 'If only that *were* possible. Conditional clause.'
Doctor Who: The Sontaran Stratagem

*

'I wish Bernard Cribbins was my grandad.'
SFX magazine, HAVING DECLARED THE FORMER
QUOTATION **BEST LINE**

Sic transit gloria…

A **transitive verb** allows the subject to perform an action on an object (see p.126 for more on subjects and objects):

She slapped his face.	She *slapped* what? His face.
He pulled the communication cord.	He *pulled* what? The cord.

✋ **Smart Alec:** Transitive verbs with one object only are called **monotransitive** (*I corrected my teacher*). Verbs with both a direct object and an indirect object are called **ditransitive** (*The teacher threw the board rubber at me*).

An **intransitive verb** acts by itself:

I sleep.	I cannot *sleep* something.
I fall.	I cannot *fall* something.

Famous intransitives

'Jesus wept.'

The Gospel According to St John

*

'Thus with a kiss I die.'

SHAKESPEARE, *Romeo and Juliet*

Just to confuse things, some verbs can be transitive when used in one sense and intransitive in another. These are known as **ambitransitive verbs**.

Transitive	**Intransitive**
*He **drank his coffee**.*	*He **drank** like a fish.*
*She **read the menu**.*	*She **read** during dinner.*
*I **gave up cigarettes**.*	*I **gave up**.*
*He **kissed her hand**.*	*They **kissed**.*

Tip: To check whether a verb is intransitive, place a full stop directly after it and see if it makes sense: *He died. You survived.* But *he hit.* (*Hit* what?) *She threw.* (*Threw* what?) A transitive verb needs an object to complete its action.

Verbal warning

Verbal nouns or **adjectives** are formed from verbs but they perform the function of nouns or adjectives, and there are three kinds of them: **participles**, **infinitives** and **gerunds**. None of these can act on its own as a verb. Instead, each helps a verb to do its job.

Participles

A **participle** is a non-finite form of a verb used with an auxiliary verb to form some compound tenses.* It can also be used in **noun**, **adjectival** or **adverbial phrases** such as:

---

* Eh? See p.75 if that was all gobbledegook.

Going to the casino is a sure-fire way of losing money. **noun phrase**, the subject of the sentence

The horse favoured by the tipsters seemed to lose interest at the second fence. **adjectival phrase**, describing the horse

She stormed out, slamming the door so hard that the mirror fell off the wall. **adverbial phrase**, describing *how* she stormed out

Infinitives

As we saw on p.71, this is the basic form of the verb preceded by *to*, but it is also used in some **compound verb forms** such as:

I was going to text you my address.
I used to go to a lot of concerts.

Or following verbs expressing feelings, or to give a reason for an action:

I would love to see her again.
Don't forget to wash your hands.
We built a fence round the garden to keep the dog under control.

Gerunds

> 'What are all these **kissings** worth,
> If thou kiss not me?'
> **PERCY BYSSHE SHELLEY,** *Love's Philosophy*

A **gerund** is a noun formed from a verb by adding *-ing*, so it looks exactly like a present participle, but is used in a different way. *When the going gets tough, the tough get going.* The first *going* is a gerund: in this sentence, it performs the same function as a noun. To test this statement, try substituting something you know is a noun:

*When **the exams** get tough...*
*When **the meat** gets tough...*

But in the second part of our original sentence, *going* is the present participle of the verb *to go*, linked to the auxiliary verb *get* to make a complete, finite verb.

Here's another example to help you spot the difference:

*I admire the girl **posing** for that photograph.*	**present participle**, referring to the girl who is posing for that photograph
*I admire the girl's **posing** for that photograph.*	**gerund**, referring to the way she is posing, but not necessarily the girl herself

Note the cunning use of the apostrophe here – it carries a wealth of meaning. And guess what? There will be lots more about apostrophes later in the book (see p.168). Oh goody, can't wait.

KIND OF FUNNY-LOOKING (OR, ADJECTIVES)

Most of us were taught the simple rule: an **adjective** is a 'describing word'. Adjectives modify nouns or pronouns. They tell us what they are like: what they look like; how big they are; and how many of them there are. For example:

*An **ugly** bug*
*A **ghastly** girl*
*A **blue** moon*
***Thirty** people*

Adjectives can be derived from proper nouns to describe such things as historical periods (*Elizabethan, Jacobean*), literary or musical styles (*Shakespearean, Dickensian, Wagnerian*), nationality or geographical location (*French, Parisian*) or other things more loosely associated with people or places (a *Freudian* slip, *Victorian* values, a *Caesarean* section). The suffix *-ian/-ean* means 'of or pertaining to (this person/place)'; *-esque* means 'in the style of (the person)': so *Dantesque, Kafkaesque* or *Junoesque*. The last of these, intriguingly, is defined as either 'of regal beauty' or 'large, buxom and (usually) beautiful', depending on which dictionary you read. Really, if the dictionaries can't agree, what hope is there for the rest of us?

Most of these adjectives are spelt with a capital letter, though *caesarean* has come a long way from Julius Caesar and is now often seen with a lower case *c*. Foodstuffs that are named after their place of origin – champagne, parmesan and the like – are another vague area: strictly speaking they are based on proper nouns, but the more generically they are used, the more it becomes 'acceptable' to drop the capital. It seems perverse, for example, to insist on using a capital *C* for *New Zealand Cheddar*, on the basis that the cheese is named after a place in Somerset, England.

A big bunch of adjectivals

A group of words can act as an adjective. If they contain a subject and verb, they are known as an **adjectival clause**. If not, they are described as an **adjectival phrase**. (No, we haven't done phrases and clauses yet, but we'll get there – see pp.137 and 142.)

*My colleagues, **who all earn more than I do,** never work overtime.*	**adjectival clause**, describing my colleagues
*He is the one person in the department **earning less than I do**.*	**adjectival phrase**, describing the person in the department

---

A fine piece of writing – or not?

It is easy to go overboard with adjectives (and particularly adverbs, see p.96). Graham Greene once wrote:

'Adjectives are to be avoided unless they are strictly necessary; adverbs too, which is even more important. When I open a book and find that so and so has "answered sharply" or "spoken tenderly", I shut it again: It's the dialogue itself which should express the sharpness or the tenderness without any need to use adverbs to underline them.'

Oh dear – what would he have made of this paragraph from *Tess of the D'Urbervilles* by Thomas Hardy?

'The young girls formed, indeed, the majority of the band, and their heads of luxuriant hair reflected in the sunshine every tone of gold, and black, and brown. Some had beautiful eyes, others a beautiful nose, others a beautiful mouth and figure; few, if any, had all... A young member of the band turned her head at the exclamation. She was a fine and handsome girl – not handsomer than some others, possibly – but her mobile peony mouth and large innocent eyes added eloquence to colour and shape...'

Discuss.

Limpet adjectives (or, Clichés)

Some adjectives are so often attached to certain nouns that they seem permanently stuck together and have become **clichés**. Please do not stick these in your writing:

absolute truth	*personal friend*
close proximity	*safe haven*
end result	*tuna fish*
free gift	*unexpected surprise*
new innovation	*work colleague*

Rule: Verbs and nouns are the 'grafters' of a sentence. They do the work. Adjectives and adverbs are the tea makers. If an adjective or adverb doesn't add anything, don't add it.

☛ **See Me After Class:** *The object is small in size, square in shape and blue in colour.*

Do not waste words on unnecessary description. *The object is small, square and blue* says it all.

REVERENTLY, DISCREETLY, ADVISEDLY, SOBERLY… (OR, ADVERBS)

> 'When it absolutely, positively has to be there overnight.'
> **FEDERAL EXPRESS SLOGAN**

An **adverb** describes a verb, adjective or adverb. Adverbs answer questions such as *how, where, when, how much, how often?*

Many but by no means all adverbs in English end in -*ly* (*almost*, *once, twice, never, well, hard, fast, soon* and *there* are all adverbs), and many but by no means all the words that end in -*ly* are adverbs (*manly, beastly* and *holy* are adjectives and *family, butterfly* and *barfly* are nouns). But it seems that in everyday speech adverbs are steadily disappearing and the adjectival form is being used instead.

The following are all commonly heard but grammatically incorrect:

*He did the task **clever** and I was **real impressed**.*
*He always drives **careful** so he won't get any points on his licence.*
*It rained **so heavy** the roof started to leak.*
*She divided them **fair** but the children still weren't happy.*

They should be:

*He did the task clever**ly** and I was real**ly** impressed.*
*He always drives careful**ly**.*
*It rained so heavi**ly**.*
*She divided them fair**ly**.*

Note that in the first example, *cleverly* is an adverb defining the verb *he did* (How did he do the task? Cleverly) and *really* is an adverb defining the adjective *impressed* (How impressed was I? Really impressed).

Ones that got away

*He doesn't play **fair.***
*I've got it **bad.***
*They're going **steady.***
*Go **slow!!***

All of these are acceptable colloquialisms, but you might think twice about using them in formal writing.

And here's an oddity: *She worked **extremely hard.** Hard* is an adverb qualifying the verb *worked* (How did she work? Hard). And *extremely* is an adverb qualifying the adverb *hard* (How hard did she work? Extremely hard). Despite the fact that *hard* looks like an adjective, we know that it is an adverb because it qualifies the verb. If you invented an adverbial form for it you would get *she worked hardly*, which just sounds odd, or *she hardly worked* which means something completely different. Go figure.

Correctly placing the adverb correctly

Although **word order** is usually important in English (see p.122), the position of the adverb is remarkably flexible. It may go after the verb, *She answered the question **hesitantly***, or it may go before the verb: *She **hesitantly** answered the question.* In fact sometimes it can go just about anywhere in a sentence:

***Scarily**, she must have been dancing too close to the cliff.*
*She **scarily** must have been dancing too close to the cliff.*
*She must **scarily** have been dancing too close to the cliff.*
*She must have **scarily** been dancing too close to the cliff.*
*She must have been **scarily** dancing too close to the cliff.*
*She must have been dancing **scarily** too close to the cliff.*
*She must have been dancing too close to the cliff, **scarily**.*

Time, manner and place

As with adjectives (p.90), a group of words can serve as an adverb, in an **adverbial clause** or **phrase**:

*I'll go to bed **when this programme has ended**.*	Answering the question *When will you go to bed?*
*I'll pick you up **just up the road from the cinema**.*	Answering the question *Where?*
*Some people do this **for fun**.*	Answering the question *Why?* – or perhaps *Why, oh why?*

That's a bit intense

Extra adverbs, used for emphasis, are called **intensifiers**: *soon **enough**, **very** nicely, **remarkably** good, **clearly** inadequate.*

But don't over-use adverbs

While adverbs can be used to great effect –

*He is **tremendously** tiresome*

*She is **fantastically** daring*
*He's **disgustingly** rich*

– it is easy to fall into the trap of using them tautologically. One way of assessing whether your adverb adds anything is to consider a sentence with the opposite:

*She screamed **loudly**.*	As opposed to screaming quietly, perhaps?
*He clenched his fists **tightly**.*	How else could he clench his fists?

These are the adverbial equivalents of *close proximity* and *tuna fish* (see p.92).

Likewise, don't fall into the trap of using words such as *fourthly*. Where possible, just keep it simple.

First, I heard a bang.
Second, I switched on the light.
Third, I grabbed a hairbrush.

There is no need for *Fourth**ly**, I checked my make-up… Ninth**ly**, I went back to bed.*

Rule: If in doubt, leave your adverb out.

DANGLY BITS
(OR, MISPLACED MODIFIERS)

> 'Eighty per cent of married men cheat in America...'
> The rest cheat in Europe.
>
> *
>
> 'Set against the murky background of gangland London
> and missing children – buy yours for £7.99...'
> **RADIO ADVERTISEMENT FOR A BOOK**[*]

Misplaced modifiers, **dangling modifiers**, **dangling participles**, **misrelated participles** – these are all expressions that grammarians toss into the conversation on purpose to confuse and embarrass the rest of us. So what do they mean? Well, consider a sentence such as:

Walking down the high street, the new shoe shop caught her eye.

We probably all know what is *meant*, but grammatically what this sentence *says* is that the shoe shop was walking down the street. The participle is dangling (or misplaced or misrelated) because it seems to relate to the wrong part of the sentence. *As she was walking down the high street, the new shoe shop caught her eye* is correct and unambiguous. As is *Walking down the high street, she was thrilled to notice the new shoe shop.*

Rule 1: The (unexpressed) subject of the participle clause – that is, the person or thing that is *walking down the high street* – should have the same subject as the (expressed) subject of the main clause: *she.*

---

[*] Not this one, we're sorry to reveal.

Rule 2: The modifying clause or phrase (*walking down the high street*) should always come as near as possible to the noun or pronoun it modifies.

Careless positioning of all sorts of modifiers can cause amusement, confusion or actions for libel:

- John still attends his local church where he was married regularly.
- We will continue to sell goods to people in plastic wrapping.
- She was taken to hospital having been bitten by a spider in a bathing suit.
- American Catholic theologians will have to wait and see the exact wording of a French document permitting the use of condoms before engaging in theological debate.
- The mother of the accused said that God would judge her son in a news conference on Friday.
- The bride was given away by her father wearing her mother's wedding dress.
- Q: Doctor, how many autopsies have you performed on dead people? A: All my autopsies are performed on dead people.

'I once shot an elephant in my pyjamas. How he got into my pyjamas I'll never know.'
GROUCHO MARX

MAY I COMPARE THEE TO A SUMMER'S DAY? (OR, COMPARATIVES)

> *Sir, Gerald Burton asks where all the comparative and superlative adjectives have gone. As far as popular television is concerned they have all been replaced by one word* – fantastic.
>
> **LETTER IN THE** *Daily Telegraph*

Comparatives (which may be adjectives or adverbs) compare two things. We say that one thing is *larger, faster, more lovely* and *more temperate* **than** another thing, or that it runs *more swiftly, more elegantly, less galumphingly* **than** another.

The African elephant has **larger** *ears* **than** *the Indian elephant.*
In Aesop's fable, the tortoise was **steadier than** *the hare.*
Shoplifting is **less evil than** *murder.*

Comparative adjectives usually employ the suffix *-er*, if the original adjective is short enough for it not to become a mouthful. If it doesn't sound right to add *-er* (*beautifuller? temperater?* Don't think so), use the modifier *more*: *more beautiful, more temperate*. And if we want to say that it is *less* ugly or *less* beautiful – that's how we do it, however short the original adjective is.*

Does it sound right? is often a good rule (the posh word is *euphony*,

---

* As is so often the case, there are subtle differences from one side of the Atlantic to the other: George W. Bush sees no objection to saying, 'We'll make America what we want it to be: a literate country and a hopefuller country.' Bush has always been a beacon of literacy and hope.

but *does it sound right?* will do just fine). *More big* when we mean *bigger* sounds just as silly as *beautifuller* when we mean *more beautiful*.

Also, there is the question of ambiguity. *The African elephant has **more big ears than** the Indian elephant* sounds as if the elephants have a collection of ears in large sizes.

☞ **See Me After Class:** Each comparison needs only one comparative: *more better* is bad, *more betterer* is even worser.

For better, for worse

As so often, it is the really common words that have irregular forms.

*The movie he took me to see was **good**, but this one is **better**.*
*The movie he took me to see was **bad**, but this one is **worse**.*
*My father has **many** mansions, but Donald Trump probably has **more**.*
*I have **a lot** of trouble with grammar, but sports commentators have **more**.*

See also **superlatives,** p.102.

Comparing like with like

Most comparatives say that something is *more or less* something *than* the other something, if you see what we mean. But it is also a comparative to say that something is *the same* (or *not the same*) *as* something else:

*He is **as** cunning **as** a fox.*
*This ring is not **as** expensive **as** that one. (I want that one.)*

That's superlative

> 'It was **the best** of times, it was **the worst** of times...'
> **CHARLES DICKENS**, *A Tale of Two Cities*

Superlatives are beyond compare. Nothing can be better or worse. They are simply the b**EST**.

*The giraffe is the tall**est** living animal.*
*Concorde was the fast**est** plane.*
*Churchill was the great**est** prime minister.*

Most superlatives end in -*est*, although not *most*. Nor indeed *worst*. And, as with comparatives, neither do longer words. Where a comparative has *more* or *less*, a superlative has *most* or *least*:

Lord of the Rings *is the **most overrated** book of the twentieth century.*
All's Well That Ends Well *is perhaps the **least performed** of Shakespeare's plays.*

Superlatives refer to more than two things: you can't be the *best* of two players, the best you can manage is to be the *better*.

> *And the **best** and the **worst** of this is*
> *That neither is **most** to blame,*
> *If you have forgotten my kisses*
> *And I have forgotten your name.*
> **ALGERNON CHARLES SWINBURNE**, *An Interlude*

> ☛ **Swot's Corner:** The Swinburne verse may be very pretty, but it's another example of poets being allowed to break the rules: *neither is more to blame*, please, Algernon!

The most worstest thing you could say

As with comparatives, you need only one superlative, so all of these are howlers:

*It is **most nicest**.*
*I think that's the **biggerest**.*
*She is the **most wonderfullest** cook.*
*He is the **bestest** foolballer Manchester United ever signed.*
*He is the **most best** footballer Manchester United ever signed.**

AND NOW WE'LL MOVE ON (OR, CONJUNCTIONS)

Conjunctions are joining words; they are used when we want to join two words, phrases, clauses or sentences together.

*Friend **or** foe*   *Sad **but** true*

*Old **and** wise*   *Rich **though** mean*

There are four kinds of conjunction: **co-ordinating**, **sub-ordinating**, **correlative** and **compound**.

---

* Though you could have *He is the most Best-like footballer Manchester United ever signed*, if you were likening a contemporary player to George Best, who was, appropriately enough, superlative in his day.

Co-ordinating conjunctions join sentences (or parts of sentences) of equal importance. They can be remembered by the mnemonic **FANBOYS**:

For
And
Nor
But
Or
Yet
So

Boys like blue. Girls like pink.

*Boys like blue **and** girls like pink.*	I'm doing no more than state a fact here
*Boys like blue **but** girls like pink.*	…which is perhaps a bit of a shame
*Boys like blue **so** girls like pink.*	The girls are doing it on purpose, just to be contrary

When a co-ordinating conjunction connects two independent clauses,* it is often accompanied by a comma: *Shall we run through that again, **or** can it wait until tomorrow?* The comma performs no real grammatical function, it simply suggests that you pause for breath. Which is a large part of a comma's job – see p.148.

Subordinating conjunctions link a main clause and a subordinate clause:

---

* Get your claws into clauses on p.137.

*I feel tired **because** I couldn't sleep last night.*
*I feel tired **although** I slept well last night.*
*I hope **that** I have made enough pizza.*
*I wonder **whether** I have bought enough wine.*

☛ **Swot's Corner:** *Asyndeton* is the joining together of two or more complete sentences without the use of a co-ordinating conjunction – *I came, I saw, I conquered* – whereas *polysyndeton* is the use of multiple conjunctions, usually where they are not strictly necessary: *His cap **and** gown **and** pen **and** ink.*

Correlative conjunctions are used in conjunction with other conjunctions:

*She owns **not only** a flat in town **but also** a country estate.*
*She plays **not only** hockey **but also** lacrosse.*
*Bob will grow up to be **either** sporty **or** clever.*
*Bob grew up to be **neither** sporty **nor** clever.*
*Bob's brother is **both** sporty **and** clever.*
*I like **both** beer **and** lager.*

Rule: In sentences such as those, decide the position of the conjunction by checking on what follows it. They should be the same construction, whether noun, noun phrase, adjective, clause or whatever. Consider the difference between these sentences:

*She owns **not only** a flat in town **but also** a country estate.*
*She **not only** owns a flat in town, she **also** rents a villa in Tuscany.*

Not only *does she own a flat in town, but her parents **also** have a country estate.*

In each case, the words following *also* 'balance' the words following *not only*. And if you are remotely interested, see the bit about co-ordination on the next page.

Compound conjunctions is a show-offy name for conjunctions made up of several words, often ending with *as* or *that*:

*I don't mind family Christmases **as long as** I am allowed to come home on Boxing Day.*
*We can go **as soon as** you finish dithering about what to wear.*
*He built a shed at the bottom of the garden **so that** he would have somewhere to keep his ferrets.*

A word on *while* and *although*

Although some grammarians argue that using *while* in the same way as *although* is perfectly acceptable, there are times when this can lead to confusion, miscommunication and other bad things that grammar rules strive to avoid.

While she was writing, her pencil broke.	No problem here: her pencil broke at the same time as she was writing.
While I like tea, I would prefer gin.	Fine, but *although* would work equally well in place of *while*.

While Cyprus is hot, you can ski.	You're unlikely to misunderstand this, but replacing *while* with *although* would remove any possibility of ambiguity.
While Sally plays the triangle, Judy sings.	Aha. Now we have genuine ambiguity. Does Sally accompany Judy's singing, or is Judy's speciality singing and Sally's playing the triangle? If the latter, use *although.*

☞ **See Me After Class:** *While Father was away, Mother seemed to have a lot of fun.* Meaning?

A bit of co-ordination

Some conjunctions have a **co-ordinating** role between two parts of a sentence, and positioning them correctly can be a bit of a minefield.

Let's start with *both. Both* goes directly before the first word of the two to which it refers. So in the sentence *I was **both** unhappy with your work and your time keeping,* the word *both* suggests that there is more than one person involved – which there can't be because there is only *I.*

The correct versions of this sentence are either:

*We were **both** unhappy with your work and your time keeping.*	I and whoever else makes up the *both* were unhappy with two things: your work and your time keeping

or

*I was **both** unhappy with your work and disappointed in your time keeping.*	I experienced two emotions

or

*I was unhappy with **both** your work and your time keeping.*	I was unhappy with two things

The same rule applies in sentences offering a choice of *either/or*.

Not *They had **either** decided to offer for the house in the suburbs or the flat in town*;
nor *They had decided **either** to offer for the house in the suburbs **or** the flat in town*;
but *They had decided to offer for **either** the house in the suburbs **or** the flat in town*;
or *They had decided **either** to offer for the house in the suburbs **or** to pay the asking price for the flat in town.*

IT'S BEHIND YOU! (OR, PREPOSITIONS)

The word *preposition* means 'something that is placed before'. **Prepositions** are usually placed before nouns or pronouns. It's their job to show where one thing is in position to another, i.e. *The cat is **on** the mat, I was **in front of** you*. Expressions such as *in front of*, *out of* and the like, made up of more than one word, are known (to the in-crowd) as **complex prepositions**.

If you are unsure what a preposition is, you might like to employ the following sentence:

The squirrel ran ——— the tree.

All you have to do is fill in the missing word. Almost any word you choose will be a preposition. For example:

to	*down*	*under*	*near*
by	*up*	*off*	*along*
around	*past*	*in*	*through*
for	*across*	*behind*	*in front of*
through	*over*	*from*	*out of*

Even *at, with* and *after* would fit – if this particular squirrel is suicidal or we're in some sort of dream sequence. Others, such as *of, between* and *before*, do not fit at all here, but you get the point.

For non-native speakers prepositions can be tricky. *I get **down off** the bus* tells us exactly what the person is doing, but most native speakers would make do with *I get **off** the bus*. However, even native speakers often think that two prepositions are better than one:

*I get **off of** the bus.* ☒   What's that *of* doing there?
*Put that **back down** on the table.* ☒
*I took a day **off from** work.* ☒

Sometimes even one is too many:

*Where did he go **to**?*
*She admitted **to** her mistakes.*
*All **of** the people present at the rally protested peacefully.*
*I'm going **down** south.*

✋ **Smart Alec:** The use of more words than are necessary
is *pleonasm* or *prolixity*.

Don't let's ask for the moon

Many prepositions are firmly wedded to other words:

*I **approve of** his choice.*
*They're **discriminating against** women.*

However, others are more loosely connected:

When I want your opinion I'll ***ask for*** *it*	…but I might ***ask after*** your health.
*They've **taken in** everything you said to them*	…but she's ***taken off*** everything except her feather boa.
*You are **good at** what you do*	…which is better than being ***good for*** nothing.

Some prepositions cause us to get our knickers in rather a twist:

absorbed in/by
*I was **absorbed in** my book.*

*All of a sudden I was **absorbed by** a giant vacuum cleaner.*

agree with/approve of
*I **agree with** your ideas.*
*But I don't **approve of** children being taught grammar.*

aim at/to/for
***Aim at** that target.*
***Aim to** arrive at work before lunchtime.*
***Aim for** Paris and try to fly in a straight line.*

among/between
*I put the cat **among** the (many) pigeons with my thoughtless comment.*
*I placed a pigeon **between** my two cats to see what would happen.*

bored of
Wrong. We should be *bored by* or *bored with* something or somebody.

centre around/on
How can something *centre around* something else? Presumably it would need to centre around another centre. Something *centres on* something – or is *based on* it.

compare with/to
*You can't **compare** my feet **to** an elephant's: they are too dissimilar to be compared.*
***Compared with** an elephant's, my feet look dainty.*

different to/from/than
Oh, don't get us started. Most manuals of British English dismiss *different than* on the basis that *than* is used in comparatives and *different* is not a comparative. Fair enough, even though many

speakers of American English would disagree. But what about different to/from? Well, many books claim that *different from* is preferable without explaining why, which is incredibly pompous and irrational and frankly just makes us want to scream *But WHY?* However, the wonderful Fowler's *Modern English Usage* (the 1937 edition, so it's not heavily influenced by computer-speak or *Friends*) says: 'That *different* can only be followed by *from* & not by *to* is a SUPERSTITION. Not only is *to* "found in writers of all ages" (*OED*); the principle on which it is rejected (You do not say differ to; therefore you cannot say different to) involves a hasty & ill-defined generalization.' Isn't that wonderful? Fowler's great.* All of which is a long-winded way of saying that you can say (and write) *different to* if you like.

made of/made from

A bit pernickety, this one, but something is made *from* something that has been transformed; it is made *of* something that is still visible or recognizable:

*This ice cream is **made from** raspberries.*	So if you don't like raspberries, have the chocolate mousse instead.
*This pavlova is **made of** raspberries, cream and meringue.*	So if you don't like raspberries, you can pick them out and I'll eat them.

---

* The best thing is that *superstition* is printed in small capitals, indicating a cross-reference – and in the article on superstition he talks about the 'havoc that is wrought by unintelligent applications of unintelligent dogma', which refers to such commonly held views as you should never split an infinitive (see p.72). Ha!

> ✍ **Smart Alec:**
> Why does your house burn up as it burns down?
> How come you have to fill in a form to fill out a form?
> Why can you see stars out but not lights out?

Get us out from under this

> 'May I end this sentence with a preposition?'
> **CHAT-UP LINE**

Rule: It is wrong to end a sentence with a preposition.*

Well, yes, if you subscribe to Robert Lowth's rules.† In Latin it is not possible to end a sentence with a preposition, so Lowth decided that this must be the case in English, too:

'This is an Idiom which our language is strongly inclined to; it prevails in common conversation, and suits very well with the familiar style in writing; but the placing of the Preposition before the Relative is more graceful, as well as more perspicuous; and agrees much better with the solemn and elevated Style.'

Perspicuous, forsooth. And note the ending of the first line, although Lowth may have been something of a wit and written this intentionally. We'll never know.

Anyway, this seems to be a rule for a rule's sake, which of course would have been right up Lowth's street. In fact, ending a sentence

---

* Or, as the hilarious grammatical joke goes, 'A preposition is not a good word to end a sentence with.'

† If you remember, he was the chap who got us into this complicated grammatical mess in the first place – see p.9.

with a preposition rarely hinders its meaning and often sounds more natural, certainly in speech. Compare:

That's the office in which I work.	*That's the office I work in.*
The choir shown on Songs of Praise *is the one with which I sing.*	*The choir shown on* Songs of Praise *is the one I sing with.*
About what the hell are you on?	*What the hell are you on about?*

'This is the sort of arrant nonsense up with
which I will not put.'
ATTRIBUTED TO WINSTON CHURCHILL

Ha-ha

Suffering from impotence, a man visits several
doctors asking for help, all to no avail. Finally, out
of desperation, he visits a witchdoctor. The witchdoctor
gives him a potion that can only be used once a year
and tells him to take it before he is ready to be intimate.
Then, when the time is right he should say 'one, two,
three' and his impotence will be cured for as long
as he likes.

The man asks, 'How do I make the
potion stop working?'

'Oh, that's easy,' the doctor replies. 'You just say, "one, two, three, four."'

That evening before he enters the house, the man drinks the potion. He surprises his wife by immediately leading her to the bedroom. Things are going well and the man whispers, 'One, two, three.'

His wife gives him a funny look and asks, 'What'd you say "one, two, three" for?'

And **that** is why you never end a sentence with a preposition!

HOLY MOLY!
(OR, INTERJECTIONS)

An **interjection** – often followed by an exclamation mark – is used to show emotion. It is not grammatically linked to other parts of a sentence.

Bah! Damn! Eek! Good Lord! God bless yer! Heavens above! Yikes! Hey! Ouch! Oh no! Poppycock! Rubbish! Stuff and nonsense! D'oh!

Well, that was easy, wasn't it? We're not even going to bother to say, 'Don't overdo exclamation marks' at this stage, because there'll be plenty of that when we get to punctuation (see p.144).

3.
SENTENCE
STRUCTURE

DO I GET TIME OFF FOR GOOD BEHAVIOUR? (OR, SENTENCES)

> 'By being so long in the lowest form [at Harrow] I gained an immense advantage over the cleverer boys... I got into my bones the essential structure of the normal British sentence – which is a noble thing. Naturally I am biased in favour of boys learning English; and then I would let the clever ones learn Latin as an honour, and Greek as a treat.'
> **WINSTON CHURCHILL**

A **sentence** is 'a sequence of words capable of standing alone to make an assertion, ask a question or give a command'. All sentences:

1.   have a subject and a predicate (see p.123)
2.   begin with a capital letter
3.   end in a full stop, a question mark or an exclamation mark

There are various types of sentence, depending on how complicated they are:

A **simple sentence** consists of a single main clause or statement (we'll come back to what a clause is shortly – see p.137): *I like pink roses*, or *You prefer white roses*.

A **compound sentence** consists of two or more main clauses: *I like pink roses best, but I expect you'll choose white ones.*

Complex sentences have main clauses and subordinate clauses: *The roses, when they finally arrived, were yellow.*

Really complex sentences (or **compound-complex sentences**, if we're going to be technical) have clauses coming out of their ears and often get a bit carried away with themselves: *The roses, which you say you ordered several days ago, didn't arrive until this morning, and were yellow, not pink or white, by the way, so the bride is not happy.*

 ✍ **Smart Alec:** The longest sentence in English literature is spoken by Molly Bloom in James Joyce's *Ulysses*. It contains 4,391 words, which makes it far too long to be quoted here, even if the subject matter were not a bit dodgy (but it is – note the use of the subjunctive there).*

KENT/INQUISITION indented taken at Deptford Strand in the aforesaid County of Kent within the verge on the first day of June in the thirty-fifth year of the reign of Elizabeth, by the grace of God of England France & Ireland Queen defender of the faith, etc thirty-fifth, in the presence of William Danby, Gentleman, Coroner of the household of the Queen, upon view of the body of Christopher Morley, there lying dead and slain, upon oath of sixteen jurors who say upon their oath that when a certain Ingram Frizer, late of London, Gentleman, and the aforesaid Christopher Morley and one Nicholas Skeres, late of London, Gentleman, and Robert Poley of London, Gentleman, on the thirtieth day of

---

* See p.84 for the subjunctive.

May in the thirty-fifth year above named, at Deptford Strand about the tenth hour before noon of the same day, the four men met together in a room in the house of a certain Eleanor Bull, widow; & there passed the time together & dined & after dinner were in quiet sort together there & walked in the garden belonging to the said house until the sixth hour after noon of the same day & then returned from the said garden to the room & there together and in company supped; & after supper the said Ingram & Christoper Morley were in speech & uttered one to the other divers malicious words for the reason that they could not be at one nor agree about the payment of the sum of pence, that is, le recknynge, there; & the said Christoper Morley was then lying upon a bed in the room where they supped, & moved with anger against the said Ingram Frizer upon the words as spoken between them, And the said Ingram then & there sitting in the room aforesaid with his back towards the bed where the said Christopher Morley was then lying, sitting near the bed, that is, nere the bed & with the front part of his body towards the table & the aforesaid Nicholas Skeres & Robert Poley sitting on either side of the said Ingram in such a manner that the same Ingram Frizer in no wise could take flight: it so befell that the said Christopher Morley then & there maliciously drew the dagger of the said Ingram which was at his back, and with the same dagger the said Christopher Morley then & there gave the aforesaid Ingram two wounds on his head of the length of two inches & of the depth of a quarter of an inch; whereupon the said Ingram, in fear of being slain, & sitting in the manner aforesaid between said Nicholas Skeres and Robert Poley so that he could not in any wise get away, in his own defence & for the saving of his life, then & there struggled with the said Christopher Morley to get back from him his dagger aforesaid; in which affray the same Ingram could not get away from the said Christopher Morley; and so it befell in the affray that the said Ingram, in defence of his life, with the dagger aforesaid of the value of 12d. gave the said Christopher then & there a mortal wound over his right eye of the depth of two inches & the width of one inch; of which mortal wound the aforesaid Christopher Morley then & there instantly died.

William Danby, Coroner of the Queen's Household (the jurisdiction where the death took place), wrote a report as follows...

With every possible respect to James Joyce and to William Danby, Coroner of the Queen's Household, a few full stops here and there might make their writing easier to read. At the other end of the scale, consider this exchange:

Going already?
I am.
Taxi, sir?
Thanks.
Goodbye.

Small but perfectly formed.

Fragments

Complete sentences need a subject and a verb. Without these, they are known as **fragments**.

That wretched dress.
Waiting in the chemist's for her prescription.
Never in agreement about anything.

Fragments need the context of other sentences in order to convey their meaning:

I had a perfectly ghastly time at the party. Sally again. Going on and on about having worn the same dress as that new actress. That wretched dress.

I saw Sally again this morning. Waiting in the chemist's for her prescription. At least, that's what she was pretending to do. I'm sure she was really watching to see if I bought anything for the weekend. Bitch.

What kind of a sentence do you call that?

Many sentences or main clauses simply make statements. The posh term for this is a declarative sentence. But they can also ask questions, give instructions or make exclamations and as such have different technical names:

A **declarative sentence**: *I saw you copying the files.*
An **interrogative sentence**: *Did you copy the files?*
An **imperative sentence**: *Don't even think of copying the files.*
An **exclamative sentence**: *How boring those files are!*

Note, by the way, that an imperative sentence doesn't need a subject. In this instance the pronoun *you* is clearly implied.

It's imperative that we have your custom

Imperatives don't have to be bossy, they can be gently persuasive, which is probably why advertisers love them:

Let the train take the strain.
Make someone happy with a phone call.
Get the Abbey habit.
Don't leave home without it.

SUBJECT VERB OBJECT

Here's a simple sentence: *I wrote a simple sentence.*

It is made up of a subject, a verb and an object. We know about verbs (or if we don't we weren't paying attention on p.70, were we? Take a hundred lines), so we can probably tell that in the above sentence the verb is *wrote*. The rest of the sentence consists of a subject and an object…

Rule 1: The **subject** is the person or thing carrying out the action in a sentence. (In this case *I*. Who wrote the simple sentence? I did.) The **object** is on the receiving end of the action. It is the thing being done to. (In this case, *a simple sentence*. What did I write? A simple sentence.) To determine the subject of a sentence, first find the **verb** and then ask *who?* or *what?* is doing the action. The answer will be the subject.

Rule 2: In a straightforward English sentence the subject will come first, the verb second and the object third.*

---

* Grammarians refer to this as SVO, but it's a term you never hear outside a book like this one, so if you throw it into conversation at a dinner party don't be surprised if people stare at you blankly and don't invite you again.

Subject	Verb	Object
Simple Simon	*met*	*a pieman*
Mary	*had*	*a little lamb*
Little Bo Peep	*has lost*	*her sheep*

Another useful piece of terminology here is the **predicate**. This is the verb and the object (or indirect object, or anything else that isn't the subject) considered together. So, in the above examples, *met a pieman, had a little lamb* and *has lost her sheep* are all predicates. So are *sat on a wall, jumped over the moon, sat on a tuffet* and *went up the hill to fetch a pail of water*. Who would have thought that nursery rhymes could prove so useful?

> 'Proper words in proper places make the true definition of a style.'
> **JONATHAN SWIFT,** *Letter to a Young Clergyman*
>
> *
>
> 'I have the words already. What I am seeking is the perfect order of words in the sentence. You can see for yourself how many different ways they might be arranged.'
> **JAMES JOYCE**

OVS or VSO?

We thought you'd never ask. The SVO rule can be broken for emphasis or stylistic effect:

| *John I can talk round* | …but James would never let me get away with such nonsense. |
| *Chicken I can live without* | …though I am rather partial to duck. |

It's also broken with questions, when the verb commonly precedes the subject: *Who was that lady I saw you with last night?*

Direct and indirect objects

So far, so easy. In some sentences, however, there is more than one object – a direct one and an indirect one.

Take this sentence: *My boss paid me a bonus.**

If you have been paying attention so far, you know that *my boss* is the subject of the verb *paid*. But now you have to ask:

| ***What** did the boss pay?* | *He paid a **bonus*** | **direct object** |
| *To **whom** did he pay it?* | *To **me*** | **indirect object** |

Hang on, you may say, how about *The boss paid me?* Doesn't that make *me* the direct object?

Well, no. The test here is to see if you can rework the sentence to put a preposition in front of the object. If you can, it's an indirect object. You could easily rephrase the above example to become *My*

---

* Far-fetched, we know, but the grammar is what matters here.

boss paid a bonus to me. Clumsy, perhaps, but it makes sense (and it would be absolutely fine if you wanted to say *My boss paid a bonus to everyone in my department*).

Don't trip up on a sentence that begins with *there* and a form of the verb *to be*. *There* is not the subject in this case: *There were lots of people out for a walk today.* To find the correct subject ask *who?* or *what?* before the verb. *Who was out for a walk today?* Answer: *lots of people.*

The exception: well, it would be, wouldn't it?

The exception to the subject-verb-object rule concerns – guess what – the verb *to be*. It doesn't take an object, it takes a **complement**. *To be*, and verbs used in a similar way, such as *to become, to seem, to taste* are called **copulative verbs** (honestly, they are – look it up in the dictionary yourself if you don't believe us) – they express a state rather than performing an action. So in sentences such as:

I am a Londoner
You became an artist
He seems respectable enough
The chocolates tasted of arsenic

the words after the verb are the complement, and they may be nouns, pronouns, adjectives or adverbs, or phrases serving the same purpose (e.g. in the above example, *of arsenic* is an adverbial phrase qualifying the verb *tasted*).

ON THE SUBJECT OF I AND THE OBJECT OF ME (OR, SUBJECT AND OBJECT)

Unlike Latin, English nouns don't bother much with cases (different endings to show their relationship with other words in the sentence) because we express that sort of thing with prepositions (see p.108) and word order. In Latin a noun would have a different ending depending on whether it was the **subject** or the **object** of the verb, and if you wanted to say *to the noun* or *of the noun*, the endings would be different again.* Then you could put the words in pretty much any order you liked and the endings would sort the meaning out for you. But English sentences such as *the dog chased the cat* and *the cat chased the dog* have exactly the same words in them and it is the order that establishes the meaning.

Pronouns don't follow this no-change rule. They do their own thing. Or their own thing is done to them.

Rule: **I = subject**
                 me = object

I is used for the subject of a sentence, that is the person doing the action.
Me is used for the object of the sentence, the person the verb is acting upon.

---

* Thank goodness we're not Ancient Romans, eh?

Not *Me telephoned Jim* but *I telephoned Jim.*	Because I performed the action.
Not *Jim rang I back* but *Jim rang me back.*	Because Jim performed the action.

Similarly: **he/she/it/they = subject**
                       him/her/it/them = object

Not *I fancy he* but *I fancy him.*	He is the *object* of my affection.*
Not *Them were responsible* but *They were responsible.*	They *subjected* us to the horror.

This rule applies, but may be less obvious, when you have a **compound subject** or a **compound object** – that is, a subject or object that consists of more than one noun or pronoun.

*John and **I*** (compound subject) *went fishing.*
He gave the bait to John (or ***him***) *and **me*** (compound object).
*My husband and **I*** (compound subject) *are both going to the wedding.*
The groom has invited my husband (or ***him***) *and **me*** (compound object) *to the wedding.*

Hint: If you are unsure whether to use *I* or *me*, or *he* or *him*, in a compound subject or object, take out the other bit: if you omit your husband from the last two examples you are left with:

I am going to the wedding (OK, you've had to change the verb from

---

*   Get it? (Oh dear – and there's worse to come.)

are to *am* because there's only one person involved now, but that's not the point here).
The groom has invited me to the wedding.

🖐 **Smart Alec:** *He's invited the wife and I* is sometimes called the **Toff's Error**, because some people think saying this sort of thing sounds posh. They're wrong. Serves them right for getting above themselves.

What's up with songwriters?

My buddies and me are gettin' real well known…
Take a good look, you're bound to see that you and me were meant to be for each other…
Me and Mrs Jones, we've got a thing going on…

Rule: the rules don't apply to songwriters. But surely they can't get no satisfaction from their writing.

Who goes there? I or Me?

*It is **I*** or *It is **me**?*
*It wasn't **I** who said it* or *It wasn't **me** who said it?*
*It is **I** who am at fault* or *It is **me** who is at fault?*

> 'Somebody's sharp.' 'Who is?' asked the gentleman,
> laughing. I looked up quickly, being curious to know.
> 'Only Brooks of Sheffield,' said Mr Murdstone. I was
> relieved to find that it was only Brooks of Sheffield; for,
> at first, I really thought it was I.'
> **CHARLES DICKENS,** *David Copperfield*

Traditionally, *It is I* is correct, because Latin rules state that subject forms are found after the verb *to be*. However, modern thinking is that this sounds rather pretentious and old-fashioned. Most people will not bat an eyelid if you say *It was me*.

If that isn't good enough for you, try avoiding the issue by rephrasing:

He can't run as fast as me (or *I*) becomes *He can't run as fast as I can*.

He's earning more than her (or *she*) becomes *He's earning more than she is*.

Or, if you aren't happy with that, just decide which way you are going to go and stick to it. This sentence – heard on a Radio 4 news bulletin recently – falls between every possible stool: *It was he who fired the gun and it was him who was killed*.

> 'Heedless of grammar, they all cried, "That's him!"'
> **REVD. R. H. BARHAM,** *A Lay of St Gengulphus*

Between you and I

Here's the **Toff's Error** creeping in again. Lots of people are anxious about using *me*. But – between you and me – it is wrong to say *between you and I*.

Rule: Always use an object pronoun (*me*) after a preposition (*between*).*

They can't take that away from me...
I've been to paradise but I've never been to me...
It's goodnight from me and it's goodnight from him.

> 'Between you and me and the grand piano, I'm afraid
> my father was rather a bad hat.'
> *The Uninvited* (FILM), 1944

My Grammar and I (or should that be 'me'?)

Few of us will have cause to ask (or answer, or give a damn about) this question in real life. However, this book does ask it, so it seems only courteous to have a go:

*This book is **about** (preposition) my grammar and **me** (object pronoun).*

***My grammar** (subject) and **I** (subject pronoun) are not on good terms.*

In a book title, we think it is safe to assume that *Grammar and I* form a compound subject (see p.127). If it was good enough for Withnail, it's good enough for us.

---

* See p.109 for a list of prepositions.

Remember your manners

If you are talking about yourself and another person, it is polite to mention the other person first.

Wishing you both great happiness from me and Giles. ☒
Wishing you both great happiness from Giles and me. ☑

I and my wife would like to thank everyone for coming. ☒
My wife and I would like to thank everyone for coming. ☑

But there's no need to be too humble –

With lots of love from the children, the dog and me.

– nor too full of oneself:

*James and **myself** went fishing.*

*James and **I** went fishing* will do very well.*

On the subject of who and the object of whom

> 'What is fame? The advantage of being known by
> people of whom you yourself know nothing, and for
> whom you care as little.'
> **LORD BYRON**
>
> *
>
> 'As far as I'm concerned, *whom* is a word that was
> invented to make everyone sound like a butler.'
> **CALVIN TRILLIN**

---

* See p.65 on reflexive pronouns for a slightly longer rant on this subject.

Rule 1:   who = subject
                    whom = object

*This is the woman **who** swallowed a fly.*

The woman swallowed the fly. The woman is the subject of the verb.

*This is the woman **whom** the fly choked.*

The fly choked the woman. She is now the object of the verb.

Rule 2: as with other pronouns, the object form is used after a preposition (see p.108):

*The people **to whom** I spoke didn't seem to know anything about it.*
*That boy **above whom** we all towered when we were at school is taller than any of us now.*
*Never send to know **for whom** the bell tolls.*

DON'T YOU AGREE? (OR, AGREEMENT)

Rule: Parts of a sentence must agree with each other. A singular subject takes a singular verb, while a plural subject takes a plural verb.

*I **was born** in a caravan.*
***She is** only a bird in a gilded cage.*
*What **were we** talking about?*
***They don't** make them like that any more.*

Straightforward enough? Less obvious, perhaps, are:

*He is one of those **men who sing** in the shower.*	*Those men*, plural, are the subject of the verb *sing*.
*A **person knows** when **he/ she is** being rude.*	Many people nowadays would say, *A person **knows** when they are being rude.* Perhaps better to avoid the issue by saying *People **know** when **they are** being rude* instead.

And what about:

*My brother **and** his girlfriend* (two people) **have** *bagged the spare room.*

*It sounds as if my brother **or** his girlfriend* (one or the other but not both) **has** *used all the hot water.*

Rule: Use a plural verb with two or more subjects when they are connected by *and*. Two singular subjects connected by *or* or *nor* take the singular form of the verb.

And another rule: *either* and *neither* are both singular. **Neither of them has** *thought about my needing to wash.* **Either he** *or* **she is** *bathing last tomorrow, if I have any say in the matter.*

Along came a distraction

Sometimes an expression may creep between a subject and its verb. Don't let this lead you astray.

The nurserymaid, *along with the cook and the housekeeper,* **has**

caught chickenpox from the children.

Poisoning, *as well as the shock of the bite,* **was** *the cause of death.*

My husband, *besides our neighbour and his dog,* **is** *walking the coastal path.*

We'll have a closer look at those parenthetical commas in the next chapter, but for the moment just note that they are precisely that – a parenthesis or bracket – and everything between them could be lifted out of the sentence without altering the grammatical relationship between the subject and the verb.

☞ **See Me After Class:**

Each *of the boys* **were** *good at grammar.*
Were he indeed?

Every *cat* **have their** *own bowl.*
No: **every** *cat* **has its** *own bowl.* Just as **every** *cat* **has** *a tail* (unless it is a Manx cat, of course, but let's not go there).

Useful mnemonic: think of these words as *each one* and *every one* and you'll remember to use a singular verb and a singular pronoun.

Rule: the following words are singular and require singular verbs:

each	*everybody*	*one*
every	*anyone*	*someone*
everyone	*anybody*	*somebody*

However, *any, all, most* and *some* can be either singular or plural. It depends whether they are being applied to countable or non-countable nouns (see p.47).

All of the petty cash has been stolen.
All of the suspects have gone to the pub together.
Some of their discarded kebabs have been discovered.
Some of the money has been found.
Most of it is still missing.
Most of the culprits are nursing hangovers.

Rule: *many, both, a few* and *several* are always followed by a plural verb.

I've got your number

Numerical expressions can be rather tricky, but just remember that the expression *the number* is singular, which means it should be followed by a singular verb:

The number is 6.
The number in question is 666.
The number of people unaccounted for is 6,000.
The number of people who died was 60,000.

Exception: *A number of* is used with plural nouns and takes a plural verb:

*A number of people **were** in shock after the incident.*

Numerical expressions, however, take either the singular and plural form of the verb, according to whether they are being referred to as a single entity or as individuals within a group.

*A million pounds **is** a lot of money.*
*A million homes **are** reported to be without power today.*
***Two** years **is** a long time to wait.*
*The **two** years since I saw you **have** dragged by.*
***Half** the people at the party **have** food poisoning.*
***The remainder** of the guests **are** still enjoying the party.*

And then there was none...

You're likely to come across conflicting views on this one. Many people believe that *none* is a contraction of *not one*, and therefore should always take the singular verb. *None* may also mean *not any*, however, in which case it takes a plural verb.

Rule: *None* is singular only when it means *no amount.* If you mean *not one* you could always say *not one*, particularly if you want to add emphasis.

***None** of the wine **was** left in the bottle.*
***None** of the drinks **are** paid for.*
***None** of the food **is** fresh.*
***None** of the people **are** well.*

How many objects exactly?

Another common area of confusion between singular and plural comes in sentences such as:

Many men cheat on their wife/wives?
The boys put their hands on their head/s?

Are we talking about bigamists as well as adulterers here? Or a number of men sharing a single wife? Many-headed boys? Or boys sharing a single head?

Rule: The two elements should agree. *Men*, plural, even monogamous ones, *have **wives***, plural. *Boys*, even non-freaky ones, *have **heads***.

Or you can write the sentences differently and duck the issue:

Many a man cheats on his wife.
Each boy put his hands on his head.*

FROM MAJOR TO MINOR (OR, CLAUSES)

A **clause** is a sentence-like construction with a subject and predicate, including a finite verb (see pp.72 and 123 for an explanation of those things). Some clauses, but by no means all, stand alone as sentences. A clause that can stand alone as a sentence is known as the **main clause**; anything else is a **subordinate clause**.

---

* When in doubt, ducking the issue always works for us.

I can't play the piano as well as my sister, even though I practise more than she does.

I can't play the piano as well as my sister is a perfectly good sentence on its own. It has a subject (*I*) and a finite verb (*play*) and makes a complete statement.

Even though I practise more than she does is not. It has a subject (*I*) and a finite verb (*practise*), but it depends on the first clause (*I can't play the piano as well as my sister*) to become a complete statement.

But it's perfectly possible for a sentence to have two main clauses, in which case they are called **co-ordinating clauses** and are usually linked by *and, but* or *or*:

*I'm going to play the piece by Mozart **and** she will play the piece by Chopin.*
*I wanted to play the Chopin, **but** she had first choice.*
*I might play in the concert **or** I might decide to go to the pub instead.*

In all these examples either of the two clauses can stand alone.

As its name suggests, a **subordinate clause** carries information that is of secondary importance to that contained in the main clause.

A subordinate clause often begins with a subordinate conjunction such as *after, although, as, because, though, if, in order to, rather than, since, so that, unless,* etc.

*Unfortunately I won't be playing, **because I've broken my finger**.*
*She won the role, **although nobody thought she had a chance in hell.***

Or it may begin a relative pronoun (*that, which, whichever, who, whoever, whom, whose, whosoever, whomever*), in which case it is called a **relative clause**.

*I used to know the spy **who came in from the cold**.*
*I used to know the spy **whom the Russians codenamed Smirnoff**.*
*I will claim to have known **whichever of the spies you bring into the conversation**.*

Which is that?

Restrictive clauses (also sometimes called **defining clauses**) define or classify a noun or pronoun in the main clause. **Non-restrictive** or **non-defining clauses** offer further description. A non-restrictive clause is usually preceded by a pause in speech or a comma in writing, whereas a restrictive clause is not. A non-restrictive clause is also usually *followed* by a pause or a comma, if it does not end the sentence.

Rule: Non-restrictive clauses are dispensable. Their role is merely to give additional information.

Sorry, have we lost you?

Let's look at some examples. Although the following sentences make grammatical sense without their subordinate clauses, they do not convey much information – the restrictive clause is essential.

*The man **who died on the trip** was once my history teacher.*
*The car **that broke down** is now in the garage.*
*You look like the cat **that got the cream**.*

Take out that clause and you are left with:

The man was once my history teacher.	Which man? Why are you telling me this? Why should I care?
The car is now in the garage.	Again, which car? So what?
You look like the cat.	Duh? I think you'll find I don't have whiskers or a tail.

On the other hand,

*The history teacher, **who had a trusty aim with the board rubber**, ensured that we never forgot important dates.*
*The car, **which broke down halfway through France**, had to be towed back to England.*
*My new cat, **which somehow got a pot of cream out of the fridge last week**, came home with someone's trout today.*

You don't feel obliged to ask *Which history teacher?*, *Which car?*, *Which cat?* at the end of these sentences. The information given in the subordinate clause is a bonus.

Now consider the difference between these:

The dogs which barked in the night-time did not recognize the thief.	**Restrictive:** some of the dogs *did* recognize the thief and therefore did not bark.

The dogs, which barked in the night-time, did not recognize the thief.

Non-restrictive: none of the dogs recognized the thief and all of them barked.

Or

I cut down all the trees which were evergreen.

Restrictive: some of them were deciduous and I left them alone.

I cut down all the trees, which were evergreen.

Non-restrictive: I've destroyed the entire forest and, by the way, all the trees were evergreen.

In both cases, the *which* in the restrictive clause could be substituted by *that*, but this wouldn't work in the non-restrictive clauses. Non-restrictive clauses are introduced by the relative pronouns *who, whom, whose* and *which*, never by *that*.

Grammarians are divided over whether *which* or *that* should be used in restrictive clauses. While researching this book, we came across all of the following in apparently respectable sources:

'Many grammarians insist on a distinction without any historical justification.'

'*Which* and *that* are equally acceptable in restrictive relative clauses; *that* is perhaps the less formal of the two.'

'Don't mix *which* clauses with *that* clauses.'

It boils down to this: if you can tell what is being discussed without the *which* or *that* clause, use *which*; if you can't, use *that*. Or, as a rule of thumb, if the phrase needs a comma, you probably mean *which*.

A paradoxical mnemonic: use *that* to tell which, and *which* to tell that.

How do you phrase that? (or, Phrases)

A **phrase** is a group of words that has either no subject or no predicate, meaning it cannot form a complete sentence on its own. You can have verb phrases (*may sink in gradually*), noun phrases (*grammatical rules*) and adjectival phrases (*even the most complicated*) but until you put them all together (*even the most complicated grammatical rules may sink in gradually*), you don't have a sentence.

Actually there are lots of other kinds of phrases, too:

Participle phrases: *having to get up in the morning is the worst part of my day.*

Infinitive phrases: *my ambition is to retire by the time I am fifty.*

Adverbial phrases: *I work a long way away, so I need to leave home before my wife.*

Prepositional phrases: *I would love to be able to stay in bed.*

But you don't really have to worry about these technical terms – as long as you remember *to set the alarm*.

4.
PUNCTUATION

PUNCTUATION:
THE VIRTUE OF THE BORED?

Actually, Evelyn Waugh said that *punctuality* was the virtue of the bored, but he doesn't seem to have said anything witty about punctuation,* so we thought we'd just paraphrase him.

Punctuation can be defined as 'the act, practice or system of using certain standardized marks and signs in writing and printing', and punctuation marks are symbols that are used in sentences and phrases to make their meaning clearer. Those most commonly used in English are the full stop (.), comma (,), question mark (?), exclamation mark (!), semicolon (;), colon (:), apostrophe (') and quotation marks or inverted commas (' ' or " ").

☛ **Swot's Corner:** Punctuation existed in Greek texts from at least the fourth century BC, although Greek and Latin scribes rarely used more than two marks, the equivalent of the full stop and the comma.

STOP!
(OR, FULL STOPS)

The **full stop** (or **full point** or, in American English, **period**) is the strongest mark of punctuation. It shows its muscle by telling us we need to make a definite pause at the end of a sentence, giving

---

* And nor has anyone else.

us time to gather our breath or our thoughts, before moving on to the next sentence. Ignore the pause and sentences run together: meaning becomes confused. Full stops are also used in (some) abbreviations (see below). They are not used:

- when we end a sentence with another punctuation mark, e.g. a question mark or an exclamation mark. *Understand? Of course you do!*
- if a sentence ends with an abbreviation. In this case, the full stop indicating the abbreviation does the job of two: *I have to go out at 9 p.m.*

From the long to the short of it

An **abbreviation** (from Latin *brevis*, meaning *short*) is a shortened form of a word or phrase that for whatever reason we do not choose to write out in full. Strictly speaking, an abbreviation is a word or words with the end(s) left off (*Prof, vol, CD, MP*), whereas one where something is left out of the middle (*Mr, Dr*) is a **contraction**, but most people use *abbreviation* indiscriminately to cover both. If an abbreviation of several words forms something that is pronounced as a word in itself (*UNESCO, radar, scuba, AIDS*), this is an **acronym**.

In British English it used to be the rule that an abbreviation was followed by a full stop, but a contraction was not. Like so many other rules, however, this is fighting a losing battle against common usage, which tends to drop the full stops unless they are necessary to avoid ambiguity. *No.* for *number* (from the Latin *numero*, and therefore strictly speaking a contraction) is frequently found with a full stop, to avoid confusion with *no* meaning the opposite of *yes*.

The full stop is also still the norm for *a.m* and *p.m.* American English tends to use more punctuation than British English and regularly retains the full stop after contractions such as *Mr, Mrs* and *Dr.*

A number of common words such as *cello, flu* and *phone* are actually abbreviations or clipped forms (of *violoncello, influenza* and *telephone*) and would once have been written with an apostrophe (or two): *'cello, 'flu', 'phone.* Some people still do this, but most would say it was old-fashioned. Some shortenings have become so accepted that to use the long form of the word would sound pompous:

Jane will not be at work today because she thinks she might have **influenza***.*

Tim works out at the **gymnasium** *every day and then catches the* **omnibus** *home.*

Pam is pushing the **perambulator** *to the park.*

On the other hand, *tache* instead of *moustache, doc* instead of *doctor,* or *gator* instead of *alligator* may be too casual for formal writing.

The theatre critic Kenneth Tynan, as an Oxford undergraduate in the 1940s, wrote *mag.* and *exam.* to indicate that he meant *magazine* and *examination.* But it is not stretching the imagination very far to think that he was being pretentious.

✍ **Smart Alec:** How come the word *abbreviation* is so long?

TAKE A DEEP BREATH (OR, COMMAS)

> 'A Comma Stops the Voice while we may privately tell one, a Semi Colon two; a Colon three: and a Period four.'
> **JOHN MASON,** *An Essay on Elocution* (1748)

Historically, the **comma** marks a short pause, a place where you might pause for breath after reading a fragment of text aloud. In grammar, the comma is used to facilitate meaning by separating the different elements of a sentence.

Some people are comma-happy; they put commas anywhere and everywhere:

Dear Professor Purvis, [comma, pause for breath]

Please may I have an extra, short, extension on my very late, and, at this point in time, largely unfinished, English dissertation?

Other people prefer to leave them out altogether:

Dear Professor Purvis

Please may I have an extra short extension on my very late and at this point in time largely unfinished English dissertation?

In the first example, there are so many pauses that it takes forever to get to the point. In the second, with no pauses at all, we risk losing the plot. How should we interpret *an extra short extension*? Is it *an extra, short extension* (i.e. a short extension in addition to the longer extension already granted) or *an extra-short extension* (an extremely short one, much shorter than the sort of extension that would usually be requested)? Just a smattering of punctuation would have helped here.

> **Ha-ha**
> (Apologies for the terribly old joke, but it illustrates the point)
> A college professor wrote on his blackboard: *A woman without her man is nothing*.
> He then asked his students to punctuate the sentence.
> All of the males in the class wrote: *A woman, without her man, is nothing*. All the females in the class wrote: *A woman: without her, man is nothing*.

So where does a comma go?

> 'We spent most of our time sitting on the back porch watching the cows playing Scrabble and reading.'

A comma can go in lots of places. Here are seventeen – count 'em – examples:

1. At a place in a sentence where you wish your readers to pause:
   Take a breather, will you?

2. After introductory words or phrases that come before the main clause:
   In 1066, the English lost the Battle of Hastings.
   Once upon a time, there lived a boy called Jack.
   Of course, … / However, … / Finally, … / Yes, …

3. Between separate clauses within a sentence:
   In the beginning, when God created the universe, the earth was formless and desolate.

4. Before direct speech:
   He asked, 'Can you tell me why I should take any notice of these rules?'

5. In addresses and place names where one part of the place name gives further information about the other:
   Ye Olde Cottage, Old Ford Road, Fordcombe.
   The President was assassinated by a gunman in Dallas, Texas (as opposed to any other Dallas).

6. On either side of parenthetical phrases or clauses (those non-restrictive bits that contain extraneous information, see p.139). These are known as paired or parenthetical commas, so there must always be two of them:
   She reversed into the bollard, which she could have sworn was not there an hour before, causing considerable damage to her car.
   One day in the near future, if we can believe what scientists tell us, this planet will run out of oxygen.

7. After items in a list:
   My favourite Victorian novelists are the Brontë sisters, Wilkie Collins, Charles Dickens and Thomas Hardy.
   In American English there would often also be a

comma after *Charles Dickens*; British English does
not generally think this is necessary.

The Oxford comma

The Oxford, Harvard or serial comma is placed before the
final *and, or* or *nor* in a list of more than two elements. (The
names are derived from the Oxford University Press and
Harvard University Press, both advocates of this usage.)
Most (British) pundits recommend it only to avoid
ambiguity.

He introduced me to Mr Brown, his teacher and his friend. (He
introduced me to one person, Mr Brown, who happened to be
both his teacher and his friend.)

He introduced me to Mr Brown, his teacher, and his friend.
(He introduced me to two people: his unnamed friend and a
teacher, whose name was Mr Brown. Or indeed, if the speaker
is particularly grammatically unaware, to three people: Mr
Brown, plus the teacher of either Mr Brown or the speaker,
plus a friend of the teacher, Mr Brown or the speaker.)

Oxford commas are particularly useful if one of the items in
a list already contains the word *and*, or in sentences such as
this one, where the items of the list are a complicated
collection of phrases or clauses. Dick King-Smith's novel
Poppet contains this perfect example: 'He asked beetles and
grubs and worms and caterpillars and little lizards and small
frogs, and some replied jokily and some replied angrily and
some didn't answer.'

For items already containing the word *and,* Wikipedia quotes *The Economist* style manual: 'The doctor suggested an aspirin, half a grapefruit and a cup of broth. But he ordered scrambled eggs, whisky and soda, and a selection from the trolley.' That comma after *soda* tells us to treat *whisky and soda* as a single item. Though from the sound of this guy, it was probably a double.

8. In large numbers. In numbers of more than three digits, use a comma after every third digit (reading from right to left):

   I make that 6,000 people.

   20,000 leagues under the sea.

   The population of Argentina is 34,663,000.

   But note that in scientific texts and particularly in tables of figures the comma is often replaced by a space: *6 000, 20 000, 34 663 000.*

9. Around a non-restrictive clause. Be careful with commas here. They change what you mean to say:

I pulled up all the flowers which looked like weeds.
Restrictive: I pulled up only the flowers that looked like weeds.

I pulled up all the flowers, which looked like weeds.
Non-restrictive: I heartlessly tore all the flowers out of the ground; they also looked like weeds.*

---

* Can't get enough of restrictive and non-restrictive clauses? We don't blame you. Turn to p.139 and ponder our obsession with horticultural destruction.

10. Before and after an appositive (that's a word or
    phrase that defines or modifies a noun or pronoun
    that comes before it):
    I, Jane Jones, declare that I was at home on the
    evening of 25 September.
    Cherie Blair, wife of former Prime Minister Tony
    Blair, was accused of not liking cats.
    And again, note the difference between:

My upstairs neighbour Bill *plays loud music.*	There could also be an upstairs neighbour called Ben, for all we know.
My upstairs neighbour, Bill, *plays loud music.*	Bill is the only upstairs neighbour.

11. Between a dependent clause and an independent
    clause, where the dependent clause comes first.
    After lunch, I felt rather unwell.
    The comma here is optional, but it does indicate (the
    possibility of) a pause for breath. However, you
    wouldn't pause for breath in the sentence *I felt rather*
    unwell after lunch, so no comma is necessary.

12. After consecutive adjectives that are equally
    important in describing a noun:
    In the dreary light of the morning, the rows of grey,
    pebble-dashed houses, with their unkempt, litter-strewn
    gardens, failed to inspire tender thoughts of home.

13. In front of conjunctions such as *like, although, but, or, so, and* and *yet* when they are used to link two independent clauses:

The show was over, but the crowd refused to leave.
It's going to be a long night, so let's get those coffees in.

Be careful with *and*, however. Unless you are a devotee of the Oxford comma, put a comma before *and* only if it introduces a new idea.

14. In place of a word that has been omitted:
The room was cold, the bed hard.

15. Before the word *too* when it means *also*:
Two pairs of ballet shoes and two tutus, too.
Parenthetical commas can also add emphasis to the word *too* if it appears in the middle of a sentence:
He'd never really thought about where to put commas in a sentence, but then, too, he'd never thought much about punctuation at all.

16. To emphasize an adverb:
I wrote it down, quickly, which is why I went to the wrong address.

17. After greetings and before closings in letters:
Dear Sir,
Yours faithfully,
This used to be a hard-and-fast rule, but is beginning to fall out of favour. Now the hard-and-fast rule is *be*

consistent: if you use a comma after *Dear Sir,* use one after *Yours faithfully,* too.

☞ **See Me After Class:** *I find writing English essays really difficult, I'm sure everyone finds that inspiration does not always come instantly, I think you'll find that is so.*

These could be treated as three distinct sentences, separated by full stops; or they could be clauses, separated by semi-colons. Or, in informal writing, if you wanted to make them sound a bit breathless, you could use dashes. But, sorry, the commas are just wrong wrong wrong.

Are you losing the will to live? Let's move on to something more straightforward.

WHAT IS THIS, THE SPANISH INQUISITION? (OR, QUESTION MARKS)

> 'To whom, then, must I dedicate my wonderful,
> surprising and interesting adventures? to whom dare I
> reveal my private opinion of my nearest relations? the
> secret thoughts of my dearest friends? my own hopes,
> fears, reflections and dislikes? Nobody!'
>
> **FANNY BURNEY**

Question: When do you use a **question mark**?
Answer: At the end of a direct question, OK?

Well, we'd probably better go into just a little more detail.

Direct questions are things such as:

Where were you when I needed you?
When did you last see your father?
Who's a pretty boy, then?

Indirect questions are things such as:

I wonder who's kissing her now.
I didn't hear what he said.
I know where you are coming from.

These sentences aren't questions, they are statements: *I wonder, I didn't hear, I know*, so they don't need a question mark.

Rule: A direct question needs a ?; an indirect question does not.

Hint: To spot an indirect question look out for the words *ask* or *wonder*, often followed by *if.*

A question in the form of a statement, known as an **embedded question**, doesn't require a question mark either: *The question whether children learn enough grammar remains to be answered.*

Hint: Look out for the words *whether* or *if* – they often indicate embedded questions.

But *The question is, 'Do today's children learn enough grammar?'* The opening words plus the comma have set the scene for direct speech, and the direct speech takes the form of a direct question. So – yes, you've guessed, go to the top of the class – it needs a question mark.

> **Note: One *asks* a question.**
> *'How much does it cost?' he said.* ☒
> *'How much does it cost?'*
> *he asked/enquired/questioned.* ☑

Rhetorical questions – questions to which we do not expect an answer – are still questions and deserve to end with a question mark. How else should we end them, after all?

Question upon question

Sometimes a question will be followed with a series of brief questions. When that happens, especially when the brief questions are more or less follow-up questions to the main one, the little questions can begin with a lower-case letter and end with a question mark. Both of the following are correct:

Who is responsible for this? The boy who cheated? The girl who told? Or the teacher who left the answers on her desk?
Who is responsible for this? the boy? Sarah? or Mrs Dean, who was out smoking a fag in the middle of the exam?

But, as so often when there are alternative ways of doing things, you should decide which style you are going to use and use it consistently.

Rule: Do not put a full stop after a sentence that ends with a question mark. But when a question ends with an abbreviation, end the abbreviation with a full stop and then add the question mark. *Do you mean 3 p.m. or 3 a.m.?*

Are you questioning my orders?

When a question is really an instruction, use a full stop instead of a question mark.

Would you take these books back to the library for me?	A polite request. Is it convenient for you to do this?
Would you take back the books as I asked you to do yesterday.	An order. You'd better or else.

SOMETHING TO SHOUT ABOUT (OR, EXCLAMATION MARKS)

> 'This stop denotes our Suddain Admiration,
> Of what we Read, or Write, or giv Relation,
> And is always cal'd an Exclamation.'
> *Treatise of Stops, Points, or Pauses, and of Notes which*
> *are used in writing and Print* (**1680**)

The **exclamation mark** may be used at the end of a sentence in the place of a full stop, in order to express strong emotion, such as excitement, delight, fear, anger or surprise.

Hey!	*Watch out!*
Boo!	*Stop!*
Woohoo!	*Run!*
Wow!	*Fire!*
Ouch!	*Detention! Now!*

It may also be used to catch the reader's attention. Compare:

Slow workmen in road.
Slow! Workmen in road.

Elephants, please stay in your car.
Elephants! Please stay in your car.

But beware of overkill. Too many exclamation marks make writing overheated. There are no real rules about using them, except *Please restrain yourself.* If you overdo it –

I'd love to! Thank you so much for asking! I'll be there in plenty of time! Oh, I'm so excited!
I'll kill you!!!!!!
Get out!!!!!
It tastes disgusting!!!!!

– you lose the impact that a single, well placed exclamation mark might have. A well written sentence should be able to pack its own punch. Besides which, exclamation marks are visually distracting and can get really annoying!!!!

Rule: An exclamation mark ends a sentence in place of a full stop and should be followed by a capital letter.

☞ See Me After Class:

'You won't give me lines will yer, miss?!'
'What is the meaning of this "?!"?'

(Answer: an **interrobang**. In formal writing, don't use a question mark in combination with other marks.)

TWO PRICKS
(OR, COLONS)

'A marke of a sentence not fully ended which is made with two prickes.'
JOHN BULLOKAR, ENGLISH PHYSICIAN AND LEXICOGRAPHER, WRITING ABOUT THE COLON IN 1616.

Rule: a **colon** informs the reader that what follows sums up or explains what has come before.

For example, it may be used to link two main clauses, where the second clause explains the first.

She was delighted to have the offer accepted: it was the third time she had bid on the house.

Or to introduce a list of items (or, indeed, an example):

The cake contained ingredients found lying at the back of the kitchen cupboard: flour, baking soda, dried peel, sultanas, raisins, brown sugar, nutmeg, cinnamon and mixed spice. To this lot, we just added some milk and an egg from the fridge.

You will need: strong footwear, waterproof clothing, a change of clothes, high-energy snacks, a small first-aid kit, a good map and a torch.

SUPERCOMMA TO THE RESCUE (OR, SEMICOLONS)

> 'There were pears and apples, clustered high in blooming pyramids; there were bunches of grapes, made, in the shopkeepers' benevolence, to dangle from conspicuous hooks, that people's mouths might water gratis as they passed; there were piles of filberts, mossy and brown, recalling, in their fragrance, ancient walks among the woods, and pleasant shufflings ankle deep through withered leaves; there were Norfolk Biffins, squat and swarthy, setting off the yellow of the oranges and lemons, and, in the great compactness of their juicy persons, urgently entreating and beseeching to be carried home in paper bags and eaten after dinner.'
>
> **CHARLES DICKENS**, *A Christmas Carol*

Now fighting a losing battle against the less elegant dash (see next page), the **semicolon** connects two or more independent clauses that don't *quite* justify being sentences in their own right. It often replaces *and* or *but*. It may be helpful to think of it as a 'supercomma'.

I have tickets for Wimbledon tomorrow. I bet it rains.	These two short sentences read a bit jerkily.
I have tickets for Wimbledon tomorrow but I bet it rains.	A little clumsy.

I have tickets for Wimbledon   Much better!
tomorrow; I bet it rains.

Rule 1: You must have a finite clause sentence (see p.117) on both sides of the semicolon.

Rule 2: Semicolons are followed by a lower-case letter, unless the word in question is a proper noun.

A semicolon is also used instead of a comma to break up items in a long and complicated list, particularly when the list has plenty of commas in it already, as in the Dickens quote above.

DASH IT ALL!
(OR, DASHES)

A **dash** (–) is a short horizontal line that may be used alone, or as a pair in place of brackets. It introduces an aside, an interruption or an additional piece of information, indicates a sudden change of emotion or thought, or shows that words have been omitted at the end of a sentence that has been broken off.*

He had said that he would marry her when he got his next promotion – and she, poor girl, believed him.
She – poor girl – believed him.
After hours of careful preparation the experiment actually worked – eureka!
They want that contract – which means they get that contract – by the end of today.

---

* Hey, there's an Oxford comma in that sentence – it must have slipped in while we weren't looking.

'He is an excellent employee, but —'

A dash can also indicate that we are carrying on where we left off:
'— as I was telling you, I wouldn't be seen dead in a ditch with her.'

Nowadays, dashes are riding roughshod over the poor old semicolon (*I have tickets for Wimbledon tomorrow — I bet it rains*), and this is becoming more acceptable, especially in informal writing.

British English usually uses an en-dash (–) with a space on either side of it; Americans prefer the longer em-dash(—) and no spaces.

A dash also sometimes takes the place of letters in order to 'disguise' swear words (does this really fool anybody?). In this case, the closed-up em-dash, or something longer, is usual on both sides of the Atlantic:

That man who hit me was a right b——d.
What's the f——g point of that?

✍ **Smart Alec:** An en-dash is named for the width of a typesetter's *n* key. The longer em-dash is the width of a typesetter's *m* key.

JOINED-UP WRITING (OR, HYPHENS)

> 'A knave, a rascal, an eater of broken meats, a base
> proud, shallow, beggarly, three-suited, hundred-pound,
> filthy-worsted-stocking knave; a lily-livered, action-
> taking, whoreson glass-gazing super serviceable finical
> rogue, one-trunk-inheriting slave.'
> **SHAKESPEARE**, *King Lear*

A **hyphen** looks like a short dash, but isn't used in the same way. Its function is to join two or more words to show that they belong to each other, and also to separate syllables when necessary – for example, when a word is split in half at the end of a line of type. Hyphens are rather going out of fashion these days, particularly in American English, but they are often useful (and sometimes essential) in clarifying meaning.

Hang glider pilots in training today.
He wore a new dress shirt and jacket to the dinner.
Fox hunting supporters.
It was a long overdue visit.
They were speaking a nonnative language.
Thirteen year-old boys sit Common Entrance exams here tomorrow.
She went through it with a fine tooth-comb.

In the above examples, common sense tells us where a hyphen would be useful. (*Fine-tooth comb*, please!)

Some hyphen rules:

- Be careful with compound adjectives. Hyphenating these incorrectly, or not hyphenating them at all, can cause confusion because we don't know which words go together: *Thirteen-year-old* boys sit Common Entrance exams; *thirteen year-old boys* would be far too young, and are an unlucky number anyway.
- A hyphen is unnecessary if other punctuation makes the meaning clear without it:
  The old English teacher was a dreadful bore.
  The Old English teacher was a dreadful bore.
  The fact that the word *old* is capitalized in the second sentence makes all the difference: in the first sentence we know that the teacher is old; in the second, it is the English that is old.

'QUOTATION MARKS'

'You are old, Father William,' the young man said,
'And your hair has become very white;
And yet you incessantly stand on your head –
Do you think, at your age, it is right?'
LEWIS CARROLL, *You Are Old, Father William*

Rule: In direct speech (when we write the actual words that are spoken) we need quotation marks. These may be single or double. Both are correct, although if you quote within speech, use double quotation marks within single, or single within double: *'I find the* government's "nanny state" attitude really irritating,' he said.

Another rule: in British English the punctuation goes inside the closing quotation mark:

'Punctuation goes inside the closing quotation mark,' I said.

'Where did you say the punctuation should go?' he asked for the umpteenth time.

'Inside the inverted comma!' I snapped.

If the spoken words end the sentence, there is no need for extra punctuation:

He asked, 'Is this the end?'

They replied, 'This is the end.'

She screamed, 'Help!'

Note that in such a sentence as *'Can anybody hear me?' she yelled'* there is no capital letter after the question mark, because it is all the same sentence despite all that punctuation.

Something to report?

Rule: Do not use quotation marks for **indirect** (or **reported**) **speech**.

They say that you can't have too much of a good thing.

He asked me how to use a comma.

What's all the fuss? (or, Apostrophes)

The **apostrophe** (') is probably the most misunderstood piece of punctuation we have. At its simplest, it is used to show possession (*his master's voice*) or omission (*you wouldn't dare*). But, of course, it isn't as simple as that.

> 'I'm sittin' on the doorstep,
> And I'm eating bread an' jam,
> And I aren't a-cryin' really,
> Though I speks you think I am.'
> **Marion St John Webb**, *The Littlest One*

Leave it out, will you?

Rule: When you omit a letter or letters in a word, you should replace it/them with an apostrophe.

If you choose to write *can't* instead of *cannot, we've been here before* rather than *we have been…*, *'80s* instead of *1980s*, or *'er indoors* instead of *her indoors*, you need to replace the missing letters with an apostrophe. Note that the apostrophe in *'80s* and *'er* tells us that something is missing from the *front* of the word, but it is still an apostrophe. Do not write *'80s* or *'er.* And if you write *rock 'n' roll rather* than *rock and roll*, you need apostrophes before and after the *n.* Don't write *'n'.* It isn't a quotation.

🖝 **Swot's Corner:** The Ancient Greeks invented the rhetorical device *apostrephein* (meaning 'to turn away'). This had nothing to do with grammar. It described the moment when a speaker turned away from the audience to address a usually absent person or a thing personified – 'O Liberty, what things are done in thy name!' This is still known as *apostrophe* today. However, over time, the word's meaning has widened to include 'something missing', such as letters and sounds.

Common contractions requiring an apostrophe include:

aren't	*hadn't*	*they're*
can't	*hasn't*	*they've*
couldn't	*isn't*	*weren't*
daren't	*it's**	*won't*
didn't	*shan't*	*wouldn't*
don't	*shouldn't*	

Such contractions aren't normally used in formal writing, unless someone's speaking, but in a friendly book such as this one they're OK. But remember – the apostrophe is replacing a missing letter, so please put it in the right place.

---

* But only when it's short for *it is*, and that's one rule even the most liberal of grammarians will insist upon. See p.69.

Thoughts on *ain't*

'Ain't ain't in the dictionary, so *ain't* ain't a word.'
(Actually, *ain't* is in the dictionary, but is still
considered by most to be bad English.)

*

'Denial ain't just a river in Egypt.'
MARK TWAIN

*

'Ignorant people think it is the noise which fighting cats
make that is so aggravating, but it ain't so; it is the
sickening grammar that they use.'
MARK TWAIN

WHAT'S NOT IN A NAME? (OR, POSSESSIVE APOSTROPHES)

At one time in the history of the English language, a common way of indicating that something belonged to someone was to add the suffix *-es*.

Singular	Possessive singular
mann	*mannes*
James	*Jameses*

At some point, however, people omitted to pronounce and write the *es*. So instead of an *e* we gained an apostrophe.

The man's hand.
James's book.

This use of apostrophes to indicate possession caught on. In fact, people started adding them to any old word, whether they carried the suffix *-es* or not.

Rule: The apostrophe is placed at the end of a noun to indicate that something belongs to someone or something. It replaces the word *of* in a sentence. If the noun is singular, add *'s*. If the noun is plural, just add the apostrophe.

The boss's chair is for the boss only.   The chair **of the boss**

The animals' feed is insufficient to last the winter.   The feed **of the animals**

Another rule: In the singular the apostrophe is always on the left of its *s*; in the plural it is usually on the right.

The school's rules (one school)
The schools' rules (two or more schools)

The princess's slippers (one princess)
The princesses' slippers (more than one princess)

What the dickens do I do with that apostrophe?

There are – of course – **exceptions** to the apostrophe rules. These are they.

1. When the plural doesn't end in *s*, add an apostrophe followed by an *s*:

> *The **men's** car*
> *The **children's** party*
> *The **mice's** lack of eyesight*

2. Names ending in an *s* should be followed by *'s* if singular and *-es'* if plural:

> ***Charles's** last name was Dickens.*
> *Charles **Dickens's** novels are well loved.*
> *The **Joneses'** standards weren't worth keeping up with.*

Our old friend euphony (see p.100) also crops up here: the moment the word becomes a mouthful, you stop adding an s. So:

> *St **Agnes's** Church*
> ***Jesus's** sandals*
> but ***Barabbas'** criminal record*

3. If the last syllable is pronounced *-iz* or *-eeze*, stick to *s'*, don't add the extra *s* – ***Sophocles'** plays* – although, with longer words, it's often easier to paraphrase:

> *The inventions of Archimedes rather than Archimedes' (or Archimedes's) inventions.*
> *The odyssey of Odysseus rather than Odysseus' (or Odysseus's) odyssey.**

It also sounds better – and makes you less likely to spit at the person you are speaking to.

---

* This rule is particularly useful if you happen to live in Ancient Greece.

4.   Then there are organizations that have simply decided
      that they are above having to employ correct grammar:
      Citizens Advice Bureau, Harrods and *Selfridges,* for
      instance. There appears to be no logic to this, but
      presumably an organization has the right to choose
      how to spell its own name. That said, ten out of ten
      for *Macy's, McDonald's,* and *Guy's and St Thomas'
      Hospital.*

But who really care's?

The problem is that, in the course of the last few decades, lots of
people have become confused about this and – rather than, as they
fear, looking ignorant by leaving the apostrophes out – they have
started putting apostrophes in where they have no business to be.
This is often called the **greengrocer's apostrophe**.*

*MOT'S HERE! FREE BANANA'S! FAIR DEAL'S! NO
DOG'S!*†
Bit's and Bob's (sign outside a south London shop)
Free Margarita's before 7 p.m. (sign outside a pub)

If the shop owners are called Bit and Bob, then all is forgiven. But
free Margarita's what? You could write *Free Margarita's lover
before 7 p.m.,* if you wanted him to get out of jail in time to go to
the cinema. However, assuming that there is no shop owner called
Bit and that margarita is an alcoholic drink, there is no need for a
possessive apostrophe in either of these examples.

---

* Oh, help – should it be *greengrocers'*?
† To be fair, only one of these is likely to be seen at a greengrocer's.

Similarly *MPs, GIs, QCs* and *the 1970s* don't need apostrophes, unless they are followed by a possessive or attribute. *An* (individual) *MP's expenses*, (all) *GIs' uniform requirements*. *A 1970s' trend* would belong to the whole decade; *1970's music* is specifically music from the year 1970.

An article in the *Telegraph* magazine was titled 'Wordsworths in Love'. Every pedant in the country started composing a 'Disgusted of Tunbridge Wells' letter. But happily the article turned out to be about the amours of both William Wordsworth and his sister, Dorothy.

Conclusion: Using an apostrophe in a plural which is not a possessive form is to be frowned on. No if's or but's.

To avoid confusion, it is permissible – but not necessarily necessary – to include an apostrophe in:

do's and don'ts   simply because *do's* looks clearer than *dos*

the three R's
No more unnecessary 999's, please
There are two s's in that word
dotting one's i's
Remember your p's and q's

But in all of these cases, it is a matter of personal taste, and the apostrophe is included only for ease of reading.

Yours, mine and ours

Rule: the personal pronouns *yours, theirs, its, his, hers* and *ours* never need an apostrophe.

*The **boys'** burgers,* but *the burgers are **theirs**.*
*The **girl's** rice cakes* but *the rice cakes are **hers**.*

The only possessive personal pronoun that needs an apostrophe is *one's*. However, be careful when using it. *One's well* could mean either *one is well* or *the well that one owns* – though with a bit of luck the context will help you work out which!

✋ **Smart Alec:** We also use an apostrophe in possessive indefinite pronouns: *Is that someone's idea of a joke? That's anyone's guess.*

What happens when two people own something?

Rule: an apostrophe is placed after the second name when the possession belongs to two people who are mentioned in the same sentence: *Jane and Peter's dog,* not *Jane's and Peter's dog.*

That one is easy because you only have to add *'s*. If, however, you – yes, you – co-owned Jane's dog, you would have to say *Jane's and my dog,* because you can't say *Jane and my's* nor, God forbid, *Jane and I's.*

✋ **Smart Alec:** *Achilles heel* is the Achilles heel here. Neither *Achilles heel* nor *Achilles tendon* has an apostrophe.

And finally…

Useful mnemonics for remembering the difference between a plural form and a singular form in need of a possessive apostrophe.

Good girls are Christians
Bad girls are Christian's

Rose's are red
Violet's are blue
Which colour knickers
Belongs to these two?

Got that? Oh good. Because we're exhausted.

5.
ODDS AND SODS
(OR, ELEMENTS
OF STYLE)

Being a bit fancy

There's more to grammar than knowing the difference between a dangling conjunction, a subordinate object and a non-restrictive apostrophe. (Or whatever. Sorry, it's been a long week.) So this chapter rounds up a few other points that sometimes cause bafflement – especially when you're trying to decide which chapter to put them in.

A big no-no
(or, Double negatives)

> 'Ther nas no man nowher so vertuous.'
> **Chaucer,** *The Friar's Tale*
>
> *
>
> '…nor your name is not Master Cesario; nor this is not
> my nose neither.'
> **Shakespeare,** *Twelfth Night*

Double negatives may not have mattered to Chaucer and Shakespeare, but they do matter in standard modern English. As Robert Lowth* put it, 'Two Negatives in English destroy one another, or are equivalent to an Affirmative.'

Rule: two negatives equal a positive and therefore negate each other. If you want to be negative, use only one.

Sometimes a double negative is obvious –

---

* Yes, him again. We did warn you – see p.9.

*I did**n't** do **nothing** right*
*I did**n't** **never** do well in that*

– while others are more elusive:

*His essay **scarcely** needs **no** correction*
*There is**n't** **nowhere** I'd rather be than here with you.*

They are all equally wrong.

> 'How can you possibly have an international agreement
> that's effective unless countries like China and India are
> not full participants?'
> **GEORGE W. BUSH**

☞ **See Me After Class:** *I ain't never 'eard of no one by no
name like that.*

But, on the other hand, when Al Jolson said, 'Wait a minute,
you ain't heard nothin' yet' in *The Jazz Singer* in 1927, he
made cinema history. There ain't no justice.

Yes-yes to no-nos

Double negatives are permissible – indeed, useful – when
they convey cunning nuances of meaning:

*It was a **not unusual** reaction for someone who has been given bad news.*	Sounds more sympathetic than *It was a usual reaction.*

I wouldn't say I don't like your new house.	I am too polite to admit that I hate it.

And they are allowed for emphasis when they belong to different phrases or clauses:

*I will **not** give up, **not** now, **not** ever.*
*You don't ask for much, **no** more than the rest of them, anyhow.*

Positive or negative?

Interpretation of a **deliberate double negative** may depend on context and intonation.

*She's **not un**attractive.*	This may mean that she is not ugly, but neither is she beautiful – she's not **un**attractive. On the other hand, we may be leaping to the lady's defence – she's **not** unattractive!
*Your visits are **not in**frequent.*	You could visit more often – or you visit regularly enough.
*I **can't not** come if you're singing.*	I don't want to come but I'm obliged to if you are singing – or I wouldn't miss your singing for the world.
*That's **not bad***	That's good – or it could be better.

Sometimes double negatives contradict themselves to make positive statements:

*I'm **not not** doing my job!*	I *am* doing my job!
*There **isn't** a day when I **don't** think about him.*	I think about him every day.
*He **cannot** just do **nothing**.*	He doesn't understand the concept of idleness.

And, guess what, songwriters use them all the time: *I **ain't** got **nobody**, We **don't** need **no** education* and *Je **ne** regrette **rien***. Although, to be fair, the double negative is completely grammatical in French, so although you can scoff at Cab Calloway or Pink Floyd all you like, don't cast no aspersions on Edith Piaf.

Ha-ha

A linguistics professor was lecturing to his English class. 'In English,' he said, 'a double negative forms a positive. In some languages, though, such as Russian, a double negative is still a negative. However, there is no language wherein a double positive can form a negative.' 'Yeah, right,' piped a voice from the back of the room.

PLEONASM, PROLIXITY AND TAUTOLOGY (OR, WORDINESS)

Wordiness – also known as long-windedness, pleonasm, prolixity, redundancy, verboseness, verbosity, windiness, wordage, verbiage, garrulousness, redundancy, tautology or logorrhoea – is to be avoided at all costs.

> 'Vigorous writing is concise. A sentence should contain no unnecessary words, a paragraph no unnecessary sentences, for the same reason that a drawing should have no unnecessary lines and a machine no unnecessary parts. This requires not that the writer make all his sentences short, or that he avoid all detail and treat his subjects only in outline, but that every word tell.'
>
> **WILLIAM STRUNK JR,** *The Elements of Style*

Imagine what Mr Strunk would have had to say about either of these examples:

'As the firemen climbed up the steps of the ladder to reach the people trapped in the building that was on fire (people with no escape!), the piercing sound of a shrill cry could be audibly heard from up high on the rooftop. Above the loud roar of the burning flames, we heard a woman screaming out at the top of her voice to the rescuing fireman. We sighed a sigh of relief when they finally reached her and she was brought down.'

'This quarter, we are presently focusing with determination on

an all-new, innovative integrated methodology and framework
for rapid expansion of customer-oriented external programs
designed and developed to bring the company's consumer-first
paradigm shift into the marketplace as quickly as possible.'

The piercing sound of a shrill cry, for heaven's sake! Give us a
break.

Rule: Be clear; be concise; be simple.

Some thoughts on pomposity

'We must have a better word than "prefabricated". Why
not "ready-made"?'
WINSTON CHURCHILL

*

'His speeches left the impression of an army of pompous
phrases moving over the landscape in search of an idea.'
**US POLITICIAN WILLIAM MCADOO ABOUT PRESIDENT
WARREN HARDING**

*

'Speak properly, and in as few words as you can, but
always plainly; for the end of speech is not ostentation,
but to be understood.'
WILLIAM PENN

*

'Clutter is the disease of American writing. We are a
society strangling in unnecessary words, circular
constructions, pompous frills and meaningless jargon.'
WILLIAM ZINSSER

A waste of space

✍ **Smart Alec:** How come *needless to say* is always followed by something being said?

Try not to punctuate your speech (and certainly don't litter your writing) with **verbal apologies** such as *and that sort of thing, as it were, do you know what I mean?, to all intents and purposes, needless to say.* Nine times out of ten, they will add nothing. Mark Twain had it right when he said, 'Substitute "damn" every time you're inclined to write "very"; your editor will delete it and the writing will be just as it should be.' The same applies to these empty phrases.

Many of us also emasculate powerful words by using them in a trivial way.* What we mean is, don't use *awfully, fearfully, terribly* or *horribly* when you mean *very.* In formal writing, keep these words for when they are needed: *He was horribly scarred by the accident.*

Er, um, room for improvement

Recent research concludes that English speakers use a meaningless word about every nine seconds and that ten per cent of English speech consists of **filler words**. And, um, you know, if you don't mind our saying so, it's sort of boring to listen to.

---

* Are you allowed to say *emasculate* these days? The thesaurus also suggested *eunuchize*, but that might be going too far.

It's déjà vu all over again…

Tautological phrases or synonyms (words that mean the same) simply repeat a meaning with different words. Making free with these weakens your writing and suggests that you don't know what the words mean. Our pet hates are *safe haven* (what other kind of haven is there, for goodness' sake?) and *PIN number* (what do people think the *N* stands for?) but we seem to be fighting a losing battle on these two. However, there are lots of other nonsenses against which we can still hold out:

absolute certainty	*factual information*	*honest truth*
accidental mistake	*fall down*	*new innovation*
added bonus	*fictional story*	*stupid idiot*
awful tragedy	*final conclusion*	*sum total*
climb up	*free gift*	*terrible disaster*
close scrutiny	*grab hold*	*true fact*
complete opposite	*end result*	*unconfirmed rumour*
eight p.m. in the evening	*HIV virus*	*variety of different*

and many, many more.

Note: one particularly common misuse is of the word *unique*. *Unique*, from the Latin for *one*, means 'being the only one of a kind', 'without parallel'. So it is (just about) possible for something to be *almost unique*, i.e. there might be two of them, whatever they are; but not for it to be *quite unique* or *very unique*.

Rule: If it is possible to cut out a word, do so.

'It was a sudden and unexpected surprise.'
BBC OLD BAILEY CORRESPONDENT

*

'Every rugby international is totally unique – and this
one is just the same.'
ENGLAND RUGBY PLAYER

Let me repeat myself

'Once more unto the breach, dear friends, once more.'
SHAKESPEARE, *Henry V*

Not all **repetition** is bad, though. The repetition of key words,
phrases and sentence patterns is obviously important in poetry.

> It was many and many a year ago,
> In a kingdom by the sea,
> That a maiden there lived whom you may know
> By the name of ANNABEL LEE;
> And this maiden she lived with no other thought
> Than to love and be loved by me.

> I was a child and she was a child,
> In this kingdom by the sea;
> But we loved with a love that was more than love—
> I and my Annabel Lee;
> With a love that the winged seraphs of heaven
> Coveted her and me.
> **EDGAR ALLAN POE,** *Annabel Lee*

And it can be effective in prose too:

> 'She turned towards me immediately. The easy elegance of
> every movement of her limbs and body as soon as she began
> to advance from the far end of the room, set me in a flutter of
> expectation to see her face clearly. She left the window – and I
> said to myself, *The lady is dark*. She moved forward a few
> steps – and I said to myself, *The lady is young*. She
> approached nearer – and I said to myself (with a sense of
> surprise which words fail me to express), *The lady is ugly!*'
> **WILKIE COLLINS,** *The Woman in White*

Of course, as with all good things in life, this can be taken to
extremes:

> If one doctor doctors another doctor does the doctor who
> doctors the doctor doctor the doctor the way the doctor he is
> doctoring doctors? Or does the doctor doctor the way the
> doctor who doctors doctors?

Say that again

A word that has two meanings that are the opposite of each other is called an **antagonym** or **contranym**.

*That horse will **bolt** unless you **bolt** the stable door.*
*The soldier was **bound** for home, when they caught him and **bound** him.*
*Having **clipped** off his baby hair, she **clipped** the curls in place in his baby book.*
*We escaped from the mudflats as **fast** as we could, before we were stuck **fast**.*

These examples are all grammatically correct, every word is used accurately, but they still manage to sound silly. Best to avoid them.

✋ **Smart Alec:** What's another word for *thesaurus*?

Choose your words carefully

As we said earlier, English is full of easily confused, similar-sounding words, with plenty of opportunity for deliberate puns and inadvertent verbal gaffes.

Visiting relatives can be boring.	Are they visiting you or are you visiting them?
I had been driving for forty years when I fell asleep at the wheel and had an accident.	No wonder; I expect you were rather tired.

Q: *What gear were you in at*   A: Gucci sweats and Reeboks.
the moment of the impact?

The former Deputy Prime Minister John Prescott was a master of this form of miscommunication – 'The Green Belt is a Labour initiative and we intend to build on it' – but while not many of us would aspire to his heights, he is an object lesson in what can happen if you don't mind what you say. On the other hand, you can have a lot of fun with words if you don't mind what you say. See what we mean?

> 'In my sentences I go where no man has gone before.'
> **GEORGE W. BUSH***

---

* Yes, him again. Where would this book – or indeed the free world – have been without him?

BIBLIOGRAPHY

Rachel Bladon, Nicole Irving and Victoria Parker,
Improve Your English (Usborne Publishing, 1997)

Ian Bruton-Simmonds,
Mend Your English, or What We Should Have Been Taught At Primary School (Ivy Publishing, 2007)

Mark Foley and Diane Hall,
Advanced Learners' Grammar (Longman, 2003)

Grammar in Practice 1 (Cambridge University Press)

Graham King,
Good Grammar (HarperCollins Publishers, 2000)

Jack Lynch,
The English Language: A User's Guide (Focus Publishing, 2008)

The Oxford Guide to English Usage (BCA edition, 1994)

Judy Parkinson,
i before e (except after c): old-school ways to remember stuff (Michael O'Mara Books, 2007, 2011)

Eric Partridge, with revisions by Janet Whitcut,
Usage and Abusage: A Guide to Good English, third edition (Penguin Books, 1999)

Tony Ramsay,
The Language User's Handbook: A Survival Guide for Students (E. J. Arnold & Son, 1989)

R. L. Trask,
Mind The Gaffe: The Penguin Guide to Common Errors in English (Penguin Books, 2002)

The Penguin Dictionary of English Grammar (Penguin Books, 2000)

Robyn Gee and Carol Watson,

The Usborne Guide to Better English: Grammar, Spelling and Punctuation (Usborne Publishing, 2003)

Other titles in the same series, all priced at £5.99:

*i before e
(except after c)*
by Judy Parkinson

978-1-84317-658-9

I Used to Know That
by Caroline Taggart and
J.A Wines

978-1-84317-655-8

*Remember, Remember
(the Fifth of November)*
by Judy Parkinson

978-1-84317-656-5